INSIGHTS FROM THE
PLAYGROUP MOVEMENT
– equality and autonomy in a
voluntary organisation

INSIGHTS FROM THE PLAYGROUP MOVEMENT

– equality and autonomy in a voluntary organisation

Edited by Ann Henderson

Trentham Books

Stoke on Trent, UK and Sterling, USA

Trentham Books Limited
Westview House   22883 Quicksilver Drive
734 London Road   Sterling
Oakhill   VA 20166-2012
Stoke on Trent   USA
Staffordshire
England ST4 5NP

First published 2011

British Library Cataloguing-in-Publication Data
A catalogue record for this book is available from the
British Library

ISBN 978-1-85856-503-3

Cover photographs: Margaret Hanton

Designed and typeset by Trentham Books Ltd, Chester
Printed and bound in Great Britain by 4edge Limited, Hockley

To the children who took us to playgroup

Juliet Baxter, who made a major contribution to the work on this book, died shortly before publication. We remember her with love and great gratitude.

Contents

Acknowledgements

Full acknowledgements for the help we have received in the creation of this book would have to include the literally hundreds of people, adults and children, in play-groups and in PPA, who have influenced our lives and our thinking for the best part of half a century.

Some people, however, must be acknowledged by name for the special help they have given to enable this project to succeed. Our heartfelt thanks go above all to Brenda Crowe, but also to Sheila Gatiss, Sylvia Leathard, Helen Smith and Joan Towle. Between them they have read drafts, created text, supplied missing facts, made useful comments and provided all kinds of sustenance. Their generosity has made many things possible and we are indebted to them all.

We are grateful also to the many people who gave so lavishly of their time, in responding to our requests by sharing with us their memories, reflections and information.

The photographs on the cover are among the many unposed special moments captured over the years by Margaret Hanton.

Foreword

Gillian Pugh

Iam delighted to be able to contribute a few words to this fascinating account of the birth and development of one of the largest and most influential voluntary organisations in Britain. New parents today probably take for granted that there will be a pre-school group or a Sure Start children's centre in their local community, but the comparatively recent growth in services for young children and their parents is in no small part due to the commitment and enthusiasm of the huge number of women (it was mainly women) who, from the early days in the 1960s onwards, came together in communities all over the country to set up playgroups for their children.

Back in 1980 my local playgroup was, for me as for many others, a lifeline. Widowed and on my own with a two-year-old, the opportunity to meet with other mothers, to find somewhere for my daughter to play with other children, to learn from being part of a group of women all struggling to bring up children and sometimes juggle a job as well – this was something very special. Before my daughter was born I had been working at the National Children's Bureau on a national study of parenting – what support was available for parents across the country as they tried to understand how children developed and how they could best support this. The playgroup movement brought all of this brilliantly together – rooted in the needs of children, centred on play and experiential learning, but also supporting parents' learning and in particular providing opportunities for women to learn on the job, about both children and themselves.

This book provides a vivid and sometimes self-critical account of the growing pains of a radical social movement – a grass-roots, community-based, 'bottom up', democratic, national organisation. It takes us from its beginnings, when small groups of women came together in their own communities, setting up and running playgroups in their own homes and in church halls and community centres, to the establishment of national and regional committees and the employment of paid staff, when there were no mobile phones and no computers, and when the only office was the kitchen table. It reflects not only the richness of the experiences offered to young children, but also the learning, friendship and personal growth of the thousands of adults who participated as volunteers and as advisers.

But at a time when government is again extolling the virtues of communities and of volunteering, it is salutary to take heed of some of the lessons in this book. It points to the importance of valuing and respecting what local people and communities say and can do, of the need for training and for financial and administrative support for volunteers. It also outlines some of the tensions that can arise between an emphasis on professionalism and high quality services on the one hand, and responding to local need and engaging with individuals on the other, a tension between national standards and local autonomy. What works for a small grass-roots organisation doesn't always translate well into the policies and procedures that are needed by a large national body, and government funding brings with it terms and conditions that can eat into independence and autonomy. And, whether at local or national level, those who know most about communities and families might lack the political skills required to steer an organisation through a shift in gear.

Financial demands and social change mean that there are now far fewer women at home with their young children with the time and inclination to run voluntary groups than there were in the 1960s. But there is much to learn from the history of the PPA, from the needs of young children to the opportunities for the personal growth of their parents, and this is an important book, both for its historical insights and for its relevance today.

April 2011

Dame Gillian Pugh is chair of the National Children's Bureau and visiting professor at the Institute of Education. She retired in 2005 as chief executive of the children's charity Coram.

Introduction

Ann Henderson

The Association of Pre-school Playgroups (PPA), the source of the playgroup movement, was founded in 1962; within 30 years it had been changed into a new organisation with different structures, different priorities and a different name. The movement continued, but PPA as such was no more.

So what? All organisations grow, change and develop. They also come and go. Why should the existence of one, relatively short-lived, charitable organisation be a matter of especial interest or concern?

The reason is that PPA was different. In several important ways it differed in structure and attitude from other organisations, including other charities. These key differences engendered a life-changing impact on the people involved in it, and created side effects that reverberate still.

One major difference was present from the beginning. When Belle Tutaev, a London mother with a lonely four-year-old daughter, set up a nursery group for pre-school children and wrote a letter to *The Manchester Guardian* about it in 1961, she received over 150 replies, many of them from people elsewhere in the country who had done the same thing.

The rise of the network

Her response to this was not the most obvious one. She could have organised a meeting for them all, or written a book about it or restricted her efforts to campaigning for state-run nursery education. What she actually did was set up her journalist husband's copier in the garage, teach herself to type and laboriously put all her correspondents in touch – not just with her, but with one another. It was no coincidence that the journal that eventually developed from this venture was called *Contact*.

By the time this very disparate group of people had decided to come together, and had then agreed to formalise their relationship by creating a new charity, the pattern was set: the members themselves were the people with the information, the power and the opportunity to instigate. This was long before 'flat management' became a buzzword; women elsewhere in the country were still battling for recognition and justice within the crippling constraints of traditional, often male-dominated, hierarchies. PPA's early members had a privileged opportunity to challenge existing systems and attitudes by carving out their own road.

They took it, and the effect was extraordinary.

The unchanging needs of young children

To our shame as a society, most decisions about educational provision for young children have in the recent past been made with the requirements of adults in mind. When women were needed in fields and factories during and immediately after the war, nurseries were provided. As soon as that need was perceived to be over, nursery expansion was no longer supported. People who regretted this decision generally did so out of concern for the adults, not the children. The TUC's *Charter for the under-fives* in 1977, for example, saw pre-school children as a hindrance to their parents' full contribution to GDP, and well-run nurseries as a practical solution to this problem.

In this respect, nothing much has changed. When falling school rolls in the 1970s encouraged primary school heads for financial reasons to admit pre-school children – often against their parents' better judgement – to school classrooms, the government of the day published explicit guidance (DES Circular 2/73) on the physical environment, programme, equipment, hours of attendance and staffing ratios needed by children under school age. These requirements were frequently ignored. In 1984, PPA joined forces with its colleagues in the British Association for Early Childhood Education (BAECE) to campaign on behalf of pre-school children against the poor practice that was becoming widespread in reception classes. Their efforts also were ignored. Despite the terms of the 1944 Education Act, the school starting age in many parts of the UK dropped, in practice, to four years. Professor Alexander's Cambridge Primary Review in 2009, with its humane and pragmatic suggestions about revisions to the school starting age, broke new ground by basing its recommendations on real research evidence about children's needs and learning – and was shelved.

PPA was different from the beginning, its very existence rooted in the social, emotional and educational needs of the children themselves. Its members fully recognised that although the needs of adults might change over time, the needs of children do not.

Children in their early years need play and they need respect.

Play is much advocated nowadays as a means to learning, and it is certainly that. It is especially valuable as a source of the early sensory experience that forms the foundation for much of our later knowledge and understanding. But play is more than that. Dr Mia Kellmer Pringle, speaking at a PPA conference in 1982, defined play as, 'the lifestyle appropriate to childhood ... the diet of the mind and the emotions as food is the diet of the body'. It was axiomatic within PPA that people caring for under-fives should have regard for play as a children's need and not merely as a means to adult-determined ends.

Respect is not a matter of sentiment. It means having regard to and validating children's previous learning and experience before starting to build on it. It means understanding the nature of parent-child attachment in the early years and establishing systems that accommodate to it. It means supporting children's self-esteem by giving them a chance to see their own parents as having status within the early years setting. It means valuing childhood as a special time with its own needs and possibilities, not just as a transit to some other stage. It means being willing to learn about children from children, by observation of them, rather than just being told about them by another adult. In this context some of PPA's earliest teaching materials, produced in 1969 with money from the Joseph Rowntree Trust, were a breakthrough model and widely used in many settings. They were silent films, completely unposed, simply showing children totally absorbed in their 'work'. Each film was designed to be shown twice, so that watchers' responses to the children and their use of materials could develop through guided discussion before watching a second time.

The motivation for adult learning

For adults as well as children, the emphasis in PPA was on education rather than mere training. Courses free of admission criteria or pass or fail systems were able to build on the students' own experiences and views of what they needed to learn, which freed many of them from the negative attitudes to learning they had acquired at school.

Formal courses, however, were not the only learning opportunity. People, mostly women, from a range of backgrounds found themselves dealing for the first time with property rental, administration and budgeting, young children's needs and behaviour, health and safety issues, local authority requirements and the dynamics of community organisations. This on-the-job learning preceded – chronologically and emotionally – any formal training in these matters. The adults in the groups, like the children, 'learned by doing'. They learned: that such learning was possible for them; that they could do things they had never dreamed of; and that they could enjoy it. It was at this point, not infrequently, that people who had left school with relief at the earliest possible opportunity started voluntarily to enrol on PPA courses.

Adult learning is much talked about now, and always with understandable associations of pleasure and satisfaction. But it is not always easy or pleasant for adults to learn. Some have forgotten many of their learning skills; some were never enabled to acquire them in the first place; some assume themselves to be incapable of learning. People tutoring PPA courses have often been saddened, especially if their own background was in education, to meet so many women brimming over with energy, resourcefulness and practical ability who seem to have spent their years in compulsory education acquiring a mental list of things they are no good at and will never enjoy. The list frequently includes many of the arts and many of the sciences.

In addition to possible blocks to academic learning, people in playgroups were hindered sometimes by issues around personal taste and good manners. Many of them would really rather not have learned to handle wet clay, recalcitrant caretakers, disreputable lavatories, unsympathetic public officials and mucky paint pots. In addition, women brought up to assume that well-behaved people should not make fusses or draw attention to themselves found it very hard sometimes to challenge entrenched attitudes, question people in authority, make demands on local councils and haggle with landlords.

Had it been simply a question of promoting their own personal development, these deterrents would indeed have deterred. What made PPA unique in the world of adult learning was that these women were not in it for themselves. They had found something that made a profound difference to the quality of their own children's lives – and, by extension, the lives of other young children. They fought for that in ways they might not have fought on their own account. Their commitment to the needs of their young children – one of the strongest of forces – drove them way past the pain thresholds of shyness, distaste and lack of self-confidence.

These powerful emotional drivers meant that the resultant learning was of a very profound kind. It did not just equip its beneficiaries with a few quick tips on laying out a playroom or writing a letter to the head of social services; it made them into different people. A Foundation Course student writing in *Contact* in 1985 said, 'I have found myself again as a person in my own right'.

This level of personal development enriches family life and society as well as the lives of the individuals concerned, and is a good reason for looking again at the open, flexible learning approaches and child-centred motivation that promoted it.

Families and the home environment

The non-threatening playgroup environment, where everybody was in the same boat and on an equal footing, often beset by similar fears of failure, enabled parents to learn on the job about the needs of young children and the ways they play and learn. Many discovered to their relief how normal their own children were just by being able to observe them in the company of companions the same age. Others were able to observe and be influenced by more benign parenting styles than they had previously managed to create for themselves.

Learning of this sort had a major contribution to make to the home lives of the families involved. Playgroup children didn't just enjoy playgroup sessions; in many cases, they went back to a different home, to parents who knew more about children's needs and were learning how to set and maintain necessary boundaries without either frightening or being frightened by their children. In 1982, a report by Gray and McMahon on 459 mothers in 32 playgroups throughout England showed more than 60 per cent of them saying, 'Playgroup helps me get on better with my child'. The importance of this function of playgroups was acknowledged by Labour minister Barbara Castle, who, announcing an increase in DHSS grant funding in 1976, said:

> The additional money will enable PPA to strengthen its activities in the deprived areas where there is most to be gained from the involvement of mothers in their children's development and in the community. This is the hallmark of PPA's success.

This 'hallmark of success' was vindicated in 1997 by input from an unexpected source: the Centre for Economic Performance, which reported on new research that had solved an ongoing puzzle. Until that time, children's social class and the levels of their parents' education had been seen as the best available predictors of their school success. However, these had never been reliable indicators, and there had always been unaccountable exceptions. Research by Feinstein and Symons (1997) now showed that these two factors were effective predictors only to the extent that they fed into one major predictor that outweighed all others: parents being interested and directly involved in their children's education.

The PPA principle of ensuring that each new generation of playgroup parents, usually mothers, took an active part in the management of the group and in sharing the work during playgroup sessions acknowledged and emphasised this crucially important aspect of early education: that parents have responsibility for and an essential role to play in the early education of their children.

This view of the young child as part of the family unit also helped PPA address another issue.

When children are very young, they need the ongoing loving support of the adults who are special to them. That is why many families with babies and toddlers make great sacrifices in terms of income and career development to ensure that at least one parent is with the children most of the time. Many parents find great satisfaction in meeting this most basic need for their young children.

But adults do also need other adults. People of both sexes who are no longer at work say that what they miss – even more than the money, in many cases – is working with a group of other adults. They miss the companionship; the shared aspirations, gripes and jokes.

Other observers of the family scene were keenly aware of the dilemma. Katharine Whitehorn, an early playgroup supporter, writing in her *Observer* column in the early seventies, shrewdly observed that, 'It was never part of the original deal for women to have babies *instead of* the rest of the human race'.

Playgroups, typically, did not so much address the problem as approach the entire situation from a different perspective. Parent-run playgroups were places to which parent and child sometimes went together. In addition to adult-child interactions, both children and adults worked and played there with their own age group, so there was no built-in conflict between the child's needs and those of the parent. In this way, playgroups provided parents with a rare and special opportunity: an environment in which adult fulfilment was not an alternative to meeting their children's needs, but a direct result of doing so. People running a group together shared successes and hard times, supported each other when there were problems, put up with each other's oddities, worked frantically hard for a purpose they shared and became, very often, lifetime friends.

Much of this adult activity was carried out with the children's knowledge, and quite often in their presence. In an increasingly fragmented society, where children's knowledge of adults' working lives is frequently limited to seeing their commuting parents leave early and come back cross, these children had a chance to experience a useful working model of adult activity.

Sharing power and responsibility

As a result of deliberate policy decisions, embodied in constitutions at all levels, nobody in PPA held too much power, or for too long. The ethos and practical implications of this radical policy are discussed in chapter 5. There was a price to be paid for it, as people who had painfully acquired valuable expertise had to hand over to people who still had things to learn. It did ensure, though, that learning continued on a very broad front. It also ensured that no single person became the unassailable source of all knowledge. Even the most benevolent dictatorships are vulnerable in themselves, and stifle both the input and the development of the rest of the population. This kind of wastefulness PPA managed to avoid, and so did the majority of its groups.

At national level, the power-sharing policy was supported by the appointment of a very small number of staff, each with a limited brief. There was no powerful 'civil service' equivalent. The elected and regularly replaced volunteers made all the decisions.

The result was a network rather than a hierarchy – or, as it was famously described in a book by a national adviser (Henderson, 1978), a series of 'cogs and spindles', mutually supportive and interdependent. In PPA, the members really did own their organisation and could change it if they felt the need to do so. The power this gave them generated levels of commitment that would be hard to envisage elsewhere.

The existence and exercise of this sort of people power was well demonstrated at PPA's remarkable annual general meetings, which came to provide a vivid and powerful image of the movement itself. They were combined with residential conferences and people travelled from all over the country to attend. It was hard to find venues that could offer residential accommodation combined with a big enough conference room. Universities were often used, but also conference centres and even, once, a holiday camp. Memorable meetings were held in a packed cinema in Wales and beneath madly swaying gilt candelabra in a windswept giant marquee in Birmingham.

We are all familiar with the manicured professional packages inviting atten-dance at the general meetings of financial organisations and some charities, where the business is bland and a quorum hard to achieve. PPA was not like that. However hard local conference organisers worked to keep costs down – and they accomplished remarkable deals – it was an expensive weekend for people earning little or nothing. Yet it was necessary to book as soon as the forms went out in late summer for the conference the following spring. There were usually about 2,000 places available and they went very quickly.

The conferences attracted distinguished speakers and offered useful oppor-tunities for comparing notes, picking up tips and shopping for bargains from educational suppliers, but the main event was the AGM itself. People went to have their say. Not only did they have it, but they also expected their say to make a difference, and it did.

This was not the result of some kind of happy magic. The reasons for it were built into the constitution and standing orders of the event. The proposals, received from all over the country and from all levels of the association, were circulated long before the meeting. This enabled people attending on behalf of their group or local branch to consult in advance so as fully to represent the views of their colleagues – who were, in some cases, helping to fund their attendance.

Members felt strongly about the issues that were discussed, and about their responsibility to the people they represented. Many, probably most, had not spoken in public before. Even if they had, over 2,000 people with passionately held opinions is a big audience for anybody. People visibly shook as they made their way to the front and were shown how to operate the microphones. But the degree of commitment and determination was so high, and the sup-port of an audience willing them to do it so powerful, that nobody backed off. They had their say.

If it emerged in discussion that the membership were not going to endorse a particular proposal as it stood, but still felt strongly that it contained elements they needed to discuss, and vote on, amendments and fresh proposals were accepted from the floor, subject to legal guidance. This opened up a whole new area of learning as people struggled to master formal debating tech-niques in order to achieve what they wanted. It was also quite a memorable learning opportunity for the person in the chair trying to hold it all together.

Being democratic does not make people – or organisations – infallible. Things did sometimes go wrong, and mistakes were made, but overall the pay-off was enormous. Over the years, PPA evolved through those long, often passionate meetings, at which the energy and exuberance of a growing membership relishing their power shaped the direction and priorities of their own organisation.

These qualities did not always make the young movement popular with the powers that be. Professor Halsey, speaking in 1978, reminded PPA that organisations challenging the status quo always risk being excluded or making enemies because they do not fit readily into other people's categories:

> It's not very easy for them to come to terms with you. You're a positive nuisance, you see. You want to do different things in different places. You don't understand about universalism and standardisation. You are bloody-minded in so many different ways that no civil servant can seriously be expected to welcome the news that they have to see the PPA in the morning.

Nevertheless, David Owen, when he was Minister for Health, insisted that money granted to PPA was 'the single best investment' in the DHSS's voluntary budget; one of the recommendations of Lord Scarman's report into the Brixton riots was the need for more playgroups; and Professor WD Wall, writing in *The Guardian* in 1984, described as long overdue:

> ... a full acceptance of the playgroup movement as an important part of official pre-school provision in this country – with an accent upon its distinguishing feature of responsible parent management and involvement, its equal partnership of specialists and amateurs in a co-operating learning situation.

There is much talk now from government at both local and national levels about the importance of the community. PPA did not talk about community; it created and became one. It created a framework capable of holding together a body of people who differed from one another in terms of social class, ethnic group and educational background, but who shared some important values and assumptions; who worked together to bring about shared aims; who related to one another on the basis of shared experience. It was not a perfect community, but it worked.

Through PPA, people had taken the initiative in meeting the needs of their own young children and of other children; they had worked closely with other adults, sometimes using formal committee structures and sometimes benefiting from informal mutual support; they had changed things, locally and at national level; they had set up and taken part in systems for the sharing of knowledge and power.

These people had a different approach to things – within their families and also in public life. They were not just passive consumers of existing systems and facilities. In a world in which inertia and indifference were already becoming major social evils, they had the skills and attitudes of active citizens. If they perceived the situation around them to be unsatisfactory, they could and would initiate change and were willing to work to bring about what they wanted. They had learned to enjoy the exercise of responsibility.

This book is not intended as either a celebration or a requiem. What we want to do, as our country approaches once again a period of massive social and educational change, is to identify those values, practices and outcomes that embody what was best about PPA, with the intention of making them available for present and future use. We must acknowledge also the errors that such organisations – and their supporters – would do well to avoid.

It is particularly important to ensure that the value and values of PPA are not lost, because they have much relevance to some of the dilemmas faced by our society today. These dilemmas include the consequences of what could be a very protracted period of financial hardship. The national debt is not the only problem, but it does make it essential for public money to be spent as effectively as possible. In addition, there is widespread concern about the quality and outcomes of our current educational system. There are also signs in some areas of a breakdown of social order, including inappropriate behaviour on the part of quite young children, and a level of social and political disaffection in large sections of the adult population that is also, in a democracy, very worrying.

In PPA, democracy worked, achieving phenomenal levels of growth and development without any top-down administration, harnessing over the years the initiative and lateral thinking of hundreds of thousands of volunteers. Playgroups achieved recognised educational outcomes for children in an extremely cost-effective way and at the same time reinforced parents' skills and confidence in exercising their responsibilities at home. The movement also initiated and extended an upsurge in adult education, especially among mature women. All of those capacities are needed, perhaps even more urgently, now.

Writing about an organisation in which power was so widely and deliberately disseminated could not readily be done by a single person. This book brings together the experiences and reflections of a group of people, all with close connections with PPA, all concerned to find ways of bringing to bear on our current problems some of the solutions that worked so well in the past.

Between them the authors of these chapters cover the quality of experience offered to children and parents, including the nature and significance of play. They make it clear that important and creative forms of play – for adults as well as children – are possible only in circumstances that guarantee at least some degree of autonomy for the child or adult involved. They also give an account of the ways in which that same essential level of autonomy, combined with the skills and experience members had acquired, enabled playgroups and the playgroup movement to develop to meet a wide range of local needs, both within the group and in the wider community.

Other chapters describe the formal and informal learning opportunities offered to adults, together with the conditions that informed and motivated adult learning, and look at the structures set in place to ensure that these were available to each successive generation of parents. Finally, the last chapters address the question of why an organisation with so much going for it ceased, in effect, to exist. The final chapter brings together the conclusions and messages from all those that have gone before and attempts to draw from them some guidelines for the future, so that the successes and failures of PPA in our generation might be of value in shaping both provision and attitudes for families and communities still to come.

1

Playgroups – a new experience
Mary Bruce

> Here is a movement which truly sprang from the grass roots of society: parents up and down the country decided that they could no longer wait for governments to provide nursery schools and began their own movement. (Joan Lestor, Parliamentary Under Secretary, Department of Education and Science, in Rachel Holdsworth: *Three Thousand Playgroups*, 1970)

No one in 1961 could have foreseen that a short letter from a young mother to *The Manchester Guardian* would lead to a nationwide self-help movement, considered by some to have been 'Britain's most extensive exercise in social co-operation since World War Two' (Midwinter, 2004).

I kept my reply to the letter secret, perhaps because of premonition that it would turn my life and that of my family upside down.

The women who answered the letter had much in common. Among the first to benefit from secondary education as a consequence of the great Education Act of 1944, many of them had stayed on at school and gone to college or university with a career in mind. When they married and started a family they usually gave up work as a matter of course. Maternity leave had not been introduced and working mothers were frowned upon. Having children meant staying at home to look after them. For many young mothers this change in their lifestyle led to feelings of disappointment, frustration, loneliness and guilt. Life at home with small children was not always as rewarding as they had expected it to be.

There were other social trends at this time that increased the strain. Employment patterns were changing, and in consequence family patterns were too.

Families more frequently moved house, away from familiar and stable communities, settling in new towns, in new housing estates which were often built with few social amenities. Sometimes fathers worked away from home during the week or were away for long hours every day. Britain's post-war recovery was developing into what we look back on now as the swinging 60s, but staying home alone all day with small children was not always easy.

Being a parent is probably the most important and most demanding role we have in life, and learning about children – what they need, how they grow and develop – is most effectively caught rather than taught, through observation and experience within the extended family and the neighbourhood. In the absence of these traditional supports, many young mothers were struggling, raising young children without family or friends nearby to model ways of coping, offer practical help and reassurance or simply take the children off their hands for a while. Playgroups were to recreate the community support that both parents and children need for health and happiness.

Women whose lives changed dramatically when they and their children became involved in a local playgroup remembered the bad times and later spoke and wrote movingly about how it had been for them. At one unforgettably dramatic moment a woman stood up at a crowded PPA conference in Scotland with her hand on her heart, saying with a strong Glasgow accent, 'See me, I was deid!'

One mother wrote:

> My fourth child had just been born when we moved to a new house on a new estate in a new town. It was wonderful for the first month or so, and then all I could think of was, where was my mother, my sister, my in-laws, my cousins? Where were all my friends? Nothing – nothing but children, breakfast, dinner, tea and quite often supper. There were measles, mumps, coughs and colds, not weeks of isolation but, with four to catch it, months. When did I have my hair done? When did I last have a lazy bath? When did I go to the lavatory with the door shut? (*Playgroup News*, Issue 1)

Another mother wrote about her feelings of inadequacy with just one child:

> I was listening to the radio one day, I think it was *Woman's Hour*, and there was some pompous man saying that if you hadn't been talking to your child since he was born he was bound to be backward in speech. William at thirteen months was a very silent child and I actually found it quite difficult to chatter away as a mum. And I just thought, I just felt, God, I've failed completely and I burst into floods of tears and felt desperate about the whole thing and couldn't cope. (Curtis and Sanderson, 2004)

Protest into action

Although the response to *The Guardian* letter signed mothers up for joining the Campaign for Nursery Education, few knew in any detail what we were campaigning for. The idea of a playgroup for children appealed, something to get involved in alongside one's children, without neglecting them.

There had been an embargo on any development of nursery education since 1960. In Circular 8/60 from the Ministry of Education local authorities were required to limit the number of nursery places to those provided in January 1957 (Palmer, 1977). Playgroup workers, lobbying MPs and local and national officials, came to be very familiar with this circular. Its terms were spelled out repeatedly in many rejections of polite requests for assistance from the burgeoning playgroup movement.

However, while the Campaign for Nursery Education petition, with its 3,588 signatures, gathered dust on a shelf at the Ministry of Education, Belle Tutaev, the author of the letter to *The Guardian*, worked at the playgroup she had set up for her own daughter and continued to reply to the growing numbers of women who had begun to follow suit around the country, putting them in touch with one another and encouraging them to let her know how they got on. Starting a playgroup from scratch was a bold venture and it was invaluable to have encouragement, advice and support from others who had just done it or were at the same stage. Belle made sure people were in touch with one another, area by area, and for some months lists of new recruits were circulated. People were inspired and spurred on by one another.

One of the ongoing characteristics of the movement was the willingness of its members to teach and learn from one another. From the earliest stage, some playgroup workers gave additional time to supporting other local playgroups as part of what soon became an indispensable team of volunteer area organisers, staffing the organisation county by county, creating an effective communication and development network.

Playgroups – a different kind of provision

In the early 60s, a new playgroup sometimes began with a letter to the local paper or an approach to parents at the school gate. At that time there were often large boards at the school gate bearing the message NO PARENTS ARE ALLOWED BEYOND THIS POINT, so mothers with prams and pushchairs gathered there every afternoon, easy targets for information of prime importance to them – a new playgroup in their neighbourhood. A leaflet, usually handmade and giving a contact telephone number, handed out with a smile, was the easiest way to pass the word around. Sometimes forming a group came about before finding a place where a playgroup might be set up; sometimes it was the other way round. Whichever way it happened it was pretty daunting if you'd never done anything like this before.

There were, of course, regulations. The legislation that governed playgroups, which were assumed to care for children for what was called 'a substantial part of the day', was the Nurseries and Childminders Act 1948, administered by local health authorities (Palmer, 1971). All playgroups, whether run in a house or a hall, had to register under the terms of the Act, even though they were neither nurseries nor childminders. Someone wanting to start a playgroup was advised to write a simple letter to the local health authority. When, in 1967, the BBC ran a series of television programmes, *How to Run a Playgroup*, and published a book with the same title to accompany it, Belle Tutaev wrote the chapter that covered registration. By this time she was the best-informed person in the kingdom about registration. She wrote:

> Reactions to the letter may vary from one area to another and even between districts in the same area. There may be no answer at all for several months, in which case phone calls to the Health Department may spur on the action. (Molony, 1967)

One of PPA's earliest publications, *The Business Side of Playgroups*, covered these matters and much else about this side of the enterprise. It quickly became a bestseller.

Surprisingly, local authorities had no legal responsibility for the suitability of the adults involved, provided that regular staff (one adult for every ten children) had a clear chest X-ray. Some authorities circulated a list of appropriate play equipment but took little interest in what went on during playgroup sessions.

The most important rules under the 1948 Act determined the number of children allowed and therefore, very often, the group's financial viability. Fees had to be low, so as not to exclude some children, but the rent had to be paid regardless of the number of children attending, so below a certain attendance level the group would be run at a loss. Numbers were strictly limited by the Act's requirements regarding the floor space for each child (25 square feet) and the number of toilets and washbasins (one lavatory for ten children and one washbasin for five). PPA campaigned vociferously against this Act from its earliest days. The Act did not apply to children of the same age in educational premises, such as nursery schools, and at the AGM in 1964 Belle Tutaev, then the Honorary President, called for recognition of playgroups by the Minister of Education to be the battle-cry for that year.

Though he continued to be polite and appreciative, the Minister of Education would not yield and each local health authority's discretion under the 1948 Act continued to cause big problems for playgroups. The regulations were designed for day-care premises and for childminders – they simply did not fit playgroups. After a long struggle there were some slight concessions. The regulators were up against mothers, who knew the toileting habits of young children intimately and simply could not understand why rules that seemed to them thoroughly unreasonable should prevent them from establishing a service that was of paramount importance to their children's needs. More-over, in some areas there were nursery classes attached to primary schools, and even some schools where children were admitted to reception classes be-fore they were five, where the level of toilet provision under the jurisdiction of Local Education Authorities, although it did not match the requirements of the Nurseries and Childminders Act, was still considered to be appropriate for children of playgroup age. PPA's magazine, *Contact*, was speaking out firmly on these matters by the late 60s:

> It is a continuing cause of anxiety to playgroups that the Ministry of Health demands one WC to ten children under five while children of the same age get along perfectly well with less plumbing in purpose-built LEA premises. Does the Department of Health realise that this is keeping hundreds of children in serious social and intellectual deprivation?

Lavatories became a national issue, with questions raised in Parliament by Joan Lestor, who became known as the MP for the under-fives. PPA eventually became so exasperated by the discrepancies between health authorities' toilet ratios that it set up a Toilet Survey of its member playgroups. This was impressively professional and became renowned in playgroup circles, some-times lovingly referred to as the 'wee survey'. Detailed results were published in *Contact* in May 1968:

> The conclusions confirmed that the needs of playgroups are more similar to those of nursery schools and classes than to those of the all day nurseries and childminders with which playgroups may be grouped in the minds of some busy health officials.

It took another two years, but a new circular from the Department of Health to all medical officers in September 1970 (DOH 25/70) did at last advise authorities registering playgroups that although they must ensure a reason-able degree of protection for children:

At the same time, they will also no doubt bear in mind the social value of much pre-school provision, including playgroups run by the mothers themselves, and the desirability of avoiding doing anything which would unnecessarily discourage a useful community activity.

This was undoubtedly a small triumph for PPA. Local authorities were still free to set the rules at their discretion, but it was progress, no doubt influenced at all levels by the rapid increase in the number of requests for registration. The playgroup movement was becoming a force to be reckoned with.

Playgroups in homes

Very few of the premises available for playgroups could be called 'suitable', the word used in the *Guardian* letter. Small playgroups in private houses were preferred by some parents for some children as a first step away from home. This preference was defended quite fiercely and home playgroups were always accepted into PPA membership.

Home groups often began just as hall groups did. A mother, sometimes qualified to work with children, had a child who was lonely, or there were other family circumstances that kept her at home. Often, there was no playgroup nearby and no suitable premises to start one. Home-based groups faced the same challenges from the registration process and had to meet the same requirements regarding ratios and safety. They also had to get agreement from neighbours and deal with the practicalities, indoors and out, of making their home into a play environment for a number of children. This sometimes entailed considerable financial outlay and a co-operative family was essential.

Some children flourished in the domestic atmosphere that was just like home, or like going to play with a friend. Home groups were often quieter than hall groups, which made conversation easier. With smaller numbers children had more adult attention and interaction, and playthings and materials were all easily to hand, so more spontaneity was possible. Outside space in the garden was a great advantage, which not all hall premises could offer. Mothers were able to settle their children gradually, often learning from observation and listening, sometimes called upon to help when needed.

A Surrey member, running a group at home, wrote as early as July 1963, describing a venture that was obviously giving her, the children and the children's parents much satisfaction:

> Although I may take ten children I have never had more than eight. Two come every day but otherwise it is two days a week. The children are very happy. The

mothers are pleased and say that it helps them, particularly if they have small babies to cope with. It has also been noticed that children leaving the group enter primary school with greater confidence than other children. (*Contact*, July 1963)

Ten years later Sheila Shinman's study of home-based playgroups revealed that very few were the money-making concerns they were sometimes accused of being. In fact they were frequently heavily subsidised by the householders. Those who ran them usually did so for a few years to fit in with their family life before returning to paid work or seeking further training (*Contact*, November 1973).

Playgroups in halls

In most of the buildings where children and parents came to play and learn, a transformation took place before they arrived and again after they left – no magic wand, but much hard labour. Many buildings were church halls, large open spaces with a stage at one end, high windows, inadequate heating and chairs in stacks around the walls. There was often a hall committee, which fixed the hire charge and the conditions of hire, but it was the caretaker whose continuing approval was needed for sand and water, paint and other messy stuff – and for more and more storage space. Playgroup workers needed diplomatic skills in all their contacts with difficult and sometimes hostile officials, but it was with caretakers that we needed them most.

The unsuitability of their premises was one of the criticisms levelled against playgroups. Certainly premises often presented huge challenges to playgroup workers.

Converting such spaces into an attractive, familiar, stimulating and safe playroom, with a range of activities that would provide children with pleasure and stimulus throughout a two or two and a half hour session, was the task each morning. Everything had to be cleared away at the end, for halls were used by different groups in the evening. Everything from climbing frames to paint pots had to be stored, sometimes carried across a yard or (more tortuously) manoeuvred underneath a stage. The task involved strenuous physical effort, but there was seldom any choice. Playgroup people grew accustomed to making-do.

There came a time, in the 1980s, when PPA was able to help. Government money became available through the Under Fives Initiative (UFI) to enable selected national voluntary bodies working with young families – PPA was one – to assist local groups financially. Most of the grants applied for in PPA were to improve premises. This was an innovative part of the UFI programme: a small grants pool to be administered by the charities themselves. It was carefully monitored by officials of the government department concerned (the DHSS), who must have been shocked to learn of the adverse conditions many playgroups were struggling with and impressed by the enormous difference small amounts of money could make.

PPA worked out conditions, procedures, limits (no more than £500) and established a *modus operandi*. To apply, groups had to be national members with a constitution, charitable status and proper financial procedures. They had to have security of tenure and no financial support apart from their own fundraising. They could apply for a grant towards bricks and mortar (outside work, floors and ceilings), heating and lighting, toilets, storage, outside play areas, equipment, overheads (rent and salaries) and, in rural areas, transport.

More than 800 grants were awarded and 262 applications were turned down. The rules were relaxed for eleven groups, who were each granted £1,000 towards purchasing their own premises, but most grants were between £200 and £250. Eleven groups returned their grant when they managed to get the money from elsewhere.

Although it created a huge amount of work for PPA, much of it voluntary because the amount of money allowed for administration did not meet the costs, the benefits were outstanding. Meeting rent increases in many cases meant groups did not have to close. Improving heating, and providing hot water and indoor toilets, enabled groups to stay open through the winter. Proper storage and more and better equipment eased the workload, made more activities possible and kept numbers up. Outdoor space gave more scope for play. Having money for small payments to regular staff encouraged commitment – valuable during this time of high unemployment. Because the effect of the UFI grant was often to improve the quality and value of shared community premises, relationships with landlords were improved.

Some non-PPA playgroups became aware that it might be worth the small subscription to belong to a national body. They discovered the importance of being properly constituted, keeping accounts and having written agreements with landlords. Standards improved; groups became sustainable. The benefits to PPA were less tangible, but just as important. Local and regional structures became closer and more interdependent; membership became more meaningful. The difficulties and triumphs of playgroups in some situations were strikingly brought home to those planning support services at other levels of the organisation (van der Eyken, 1987).

The UFI money made many groups viable but it did not make them rich. Much of the play equipment provided for the children in playgroups was home-made, second-hand or improvised, or bought new as a result of collaborative fundraising. Looking back with hindsight from the vantage point of an increasingly wasteful society that is now heavily in debt, the children in playgroups were in this way presented with a model that might well have more long-term value than the current one.

Playgroups – parents in working co-operatives

In the 1960s, when an individual or a group of parents decided to explore the possibility of a local playgroup, there was of course no money. Fundraising was a first step and often began well in advance of the playgroup opening. As people came together to organise events, to beg or borrow equipment and materials and to work out ways of improvising, they got to know one another, discovering each other's strengths and weaknesses.

It could be said that the camaraderie of playgroups and of the playgroup movement often began at this point. The excitement and stimulation of working together for the children, often against enormous odds, engendered a spirit that remained a driving force within PPA for many years. Such spirit pervaded the organisation at all levels. It was something visiting speakers often remarked on at national conferences – which were, just like playgroups, organised by playgroup people themselves.

The *Guardian* letter had recommended employing teachers, who might be at home while their children were young, to take charge. Some groups advertised and waited until a suitably trained person in the right place at the right time responded. Sometimes a teacher with young children of playgroup age took the initiative herself. It was often a case of one person emerging prepared to give a lead to a team of helpers to get a project off the ground, just as Belle Tutaev had done.

There was never enough money for a salary, otherwise fees would have had to be prohibitive. A free place at playgroup for one's child was the usual arrangement for mothers who helped, at least until the group was up and running. I remember the two of us who worked together in charge at our playgroup eventually asking the committee if we might have a small token payment which would enable us to take our family washing to the launderette!

This unsophisticated interdependence among a group of parents had at least three very important consequences:

First, the playgroup was always ours – a community affair – and never *mine* in the sense that her classroom at school belonged to the teacher. To begin with we had found the place, gathered the group, raised and spent the money, donated much of the equipment, decided how the enterprise was to be run. Everyone had a stake in it. As time went on, we had to work out how we could keep it that way. People joining had to know that if they wanted a place for their child they would have to help. There was a long list of jobs to be done. Everyone had at least one job. Fundraising was essential and events to raise money provided a social life around the playgroup. There were many rewards and much satisfaction, one of the greatest being able to watch how the children benefited.

Second, the very existence of the playroom ready and waiting each morning depended on parent co-operation. There was never any doubt that parents were needed; it could not happen without them. There were rotas. Mothers took it in turns to come early to arrange the room, to stay late and clear up after everyone had gone. Each mother, once a month or so, stayed all morning. That way, everyone got to know how things were arranged, how they were put away, what the routine was. There was always someone to show new people how things were done. One small boy, holding his mother's hand tight as she took him to school on his first morning, asked her, 'When will it be your turn to help?' Surprised, his mother said, 'Oh, it's not like playgroup. Mothers don't come in to help at school. There's just one teacher'. 'One teacher?' He looked up at her in amazement. 'She'll never manage!' he said.

Third, because we had no previous knowledge of how to do it, we had to learn, fast and urgently, and this learning played back into our homes and into our relationships, particularly our relationships with our children. We learned by simply being there, watching and listening. Seeing one's own child alongside others could be fascinating; much of what seemed worrying at home we saw was normal growing up behaviour and would pass. We learned how to be with children, how to listen, how to talk, getting down to their level, how to pace things. We observed behaviour: that play was a serious affair, a child's work, to be respected and provided for at home with simple activities, not necessarily expensive toys.

Fathers helped too, though usually behind the scenes, especially looking after things at home when their wives were out in the evenings or at weekends. The playgroup movement could not have happened as it did without the co-operation of men who adjusted to the changes in their home life, recognising the contribution their wives were making to their children's development through this active and often demanding community work.

Fathers helped playgroups most often by fetching and carrying, mending and creating equipment which was much too expensive to purchase: low folding tables, painting easels, dolls' beds, climbing frames, shop counters, pretend kitchen stoves, wooden building materials. Unless working shifts, they were seldom able to see their children in action at playgroup, though some fathers attended on their days off.

When they were available during the playgroup session, fathers could provide a valuable addition to the range of adult resources available to the children. Big boys sometimes presented a challenge, especially if there was no outdoor play-space, which was often the case. Having been at playgroup for several terms, four-year-old boys had reached the stage of beginning to 'play like men' as one playgroup course tutor put it, sometimes in small gangs, which could make heavy demands on play leaders with limited space and limited resources – and with smaller children with different needs looking on, and no doubt learning how it would be when they were four!

There was nothing deviant about this behaviour but it called for particular understanding and consideration. Having a male helper to work with the boys on appropriately chosen activities could make a significant difference. Teenage boys on work experience were particularly welcome, and fathers on shift work could sometimes be persuaded to stay for a morning. Divorced fathers, with custody of their young children at weekends, often living in rented rooms, with little money for outings or treats, found a Saturday morning playgroup in a local hall, with a father as one of the helpers, met a real need.

Advice and support from the national organisation

Over the years *Contact*, PPA's monthly journal, became a lifeline for playgroup workers, who gained and shared experience and knowledge through this essentially practical publication, as well as through the support of area organisers and, increasingly as time went on, through getting together to talk shop. We seemed to be learning all the time.

From the very first issues, *Contact* ran regular features:

- ☐ enabling practitioners to share ideas and successes with one another
- ☐ publishing authoritative advice from professionals in the field
- ☐ encouraging members to air their views and to challenge accepted assumptions
- ☐ testing and recommending equipment

☐ keeping members in touch with the efforts their elected representatives were making on their behalf.

From the late 1960s the magazine grew more substantial and increasingly readable and attractive. Now printed, with colourful covers and line drawings, sometimes even photographs, *Contact* was the voice of PPA. Special issues raised a wide spectrum of interests, including rising fives, disabled children, rural playgroups, multiracial playgroups, science, those big boys, paint and junk.

Similarly, PPA publications, all written and illustrated by PPA volunteers, reflected changing needs as the organisation, in close touch through its expanding network, became aware of anxieties and difficulties. At first they covered basic information about getting started: *Starting a Playgroup, Playgroup Activities, The Business Side of Playgroups* and *The Supervisor's Handbook.* Later they shared growing expertise: *Settling a Child into a Playgroup, Stories to Tell* and *Parents in Playgroups.* Some helped with publicity and public relations: *Why Playgroups?* and *Playgroups at Work.*

Publications for parents
Members of PPA were able to order publications in bulk at bargain rates in order to arrange displays at local meetings, where they attracted attention from parents as yet uninvolved in playgroups. Such parents were potentially a wider audience for PPA, and PPA's *Playgroup News*, a newspaper for the whole family, from its launch in 1969 reached out to them with stories and pictures from what was now a national network about to launch its first National Playgroup Week.

The newsprint of *Playgroup News* was succeeded in 1975 by *Under Five*, a colourful quarterly magazine for parents and families in playgroups. These publications were just one expression of the organisation's commitment from the beginning to the essential role of parents in PPA. Another aspect of the same commitment was the deliberate accessibility of all PPA publications. Practical, down-to-earth and jargon-free, they could be read and used by anybody and many parents bought for home use the ever-expanding range of publications about aspects of young children's play.

Values and standards
Some professionals denigrated playgroups on the grounds that parents, operating in not very suitable public buildings, could not possibly achieve high standards of provision for the children. It was natural that they should be concerned about standards. PPA was concerned about standards too.

To address this concern, PPA and the Nursery Schools Association began to discuss the idea of nursery professionals visiting and inspecting playgroups on an area basis as part of an Approved Group Scheme. Plans for such a scheme demonstrated PPA's concern for quality – a good political move, though it caused controversy in the ranks, some groups seeing it as potentially divisive.

Careful consideration about how the scheme was to be organised had to be set aside while the administration dealt with an avalanche of membership applications from new playgroups. The planning process was then overtaken by a number of factors: events, changes of personnel and priorities and sheer pressure of responsibilities and work.

There were also, however, the beginnings of an important change in emphasis. Closer contact with area organisers, together with feedback to the national committee following the first national adviser's visits to playgroups in her first six months, gave pause for thought. Her discerning reports on what she was finding helped to discriminate between value and standard and to recognise that advice and support were more appropriate and urgent at this time than inspection. An objective assessment of the standards of premises, equipment and even interactions in a playgroup, she pointed out, might not adequately reflect the group's value in changing for the better the lives and expectations of the parents and children playing and working there. Eventually the scheme was shelved. It seems unlikely that local education authorities would in any case have released scarce nursery school staff to visit groups that were still the responsibility of the health authorities.

One important role for the developing national body was to smooth the way for local developments by means of national negotiations. The hall playgroups' relationships with their landlords had often been a cause of stress and in the early 80s PPA approached two national organisations concerned with community associations and village halls: the National Federation of Community Associations and the Village Halls Advisory Service. After a very useful exchange of information, both organisations recommended to their members the value of playgroup representation on hall committees as important user groups. PPA groups were highly regarded as hall users by the representatives of both organisations and it was made quite clear that PPA groups using halls were fully entitled to retain their own constitutions and to operate as individual charities.

PPA at local level

In 1967 The Central Advisory Council for Education's Plowden Report on Primary Education had a section of great interest to PPA. It recommended that until such time as nursery groups could be provided by the maintained sector, local education authorities should be given power and should be encouraged to give financial and other assistance to non-profit making associations which in their opinion filled a need which could not otherwise be met. This meant in practice that although health departments and later, after the Seebohm Report, social services departments remained responsible for registering premises, education departments were now able to take an interest in and help playgroups.

PPA lost no time in pursuing these new opportunities for increased resources. From this point the creation of playgroup adviser posts at county and metropolitan area level began to multiply, each appointment a milestone marking increasing recognition and understanding by local authorities of the value of playgroups.

ILEA (the Inner London Education Authority) had already given a grant to PPA, as early as 1964, to appoint a part-time organiser. At that time there were over 80 playgroups in Inner London and this appointment hastened the need for Inner London members to form their own organisation, adopting a constitution in 1967 and ensuring close contacts through membership with the national body. Inner London PPA pioneered courses for playgroup people at Morley College and other centres in London, and playgroup development in the capital was very soon the envy of the rest of the country.

Supported by ILEA, Inner London PPA was adventurous and experimental in developing strategies to support playgroups, recognising their unique contribution. Inspired by the Plowden Report, they developed a scheme whereby a teacher would be employed to support a cluster of three playgroups, working as an assistant in each group in turn, so that each might benefit from her deeper knowledge of child development and her wider experience of presenting play activities, but leaving unchanged the basic structure of each group. Each group would continue to be run by the parents, and the play sessions would continue to be the responsibility of the play leader. This was extending and rewarding financially the work voluntary area organisers were doing elsewhere. Another much earlier initiative, capitalising on local resources in a way that became characteristic of the playgroup movement, was co-operation with the London Parks Department to set up one o'clock clubs, outdoor fenced-off playgroups for under-fives and their parents.

Increasingly across the country playgroups had begun to work together as PPA branches. This caused anxiety at first, until roles and relationships were agreed and a branch constitution approved. There were seven branches by 1964, and a voluntary branches officer was appointed to deal with enquiries concerning organisation and development. Far from undermining the national body's usefulness and its income from subscriptions, as had been feared, branches quickly proved a great asset. They published regular newsletters, full of vital information about what was going on locally under PPA's umbrella. One of the biggest difficulties in the early years was keeping abreast of rapidly expanding local experience, as busy local activists found it difficult to take time out to report. Branch secretaries now became, with area organisers, key figures in the chain of communication, with the result that the national committee was better informed.

Working at branch level was rewarding. Parents came together to support playgroups and each other, to reach a fuller understanding of what was involved and why it was important, to raise money and to lobby those with influence. Local newsletters, public meetings, joint approaches to local authorities and publicity stunts that attracted local press coverage all generated co-operation, friendship and fun.

A playgroup in a shop window in Croydon inspired Harrow Branch to copy the idea and to run a group for a week in the largest department store in the town. The children just got on with it and the onlookers were entranced and learned a little about what was going on and why. Ipswich and District Branch mounted a similar publicity stunt in Co-op stores in the summer of 1967. Relays of committee members handed out literature and by the end of the week Ipswich people knew a lot more than they had before about what playgroups were and what they were achieving.

In Southampton a few years later, the local authority worked with the local PPA branch to fix a sheet of stiff white plastic round the outside of the building that housed the Civic Centre, the library and the art gallery. Branch committee members spent a Saturday handing out big brushes and paint pots to children and parents who between them during the course of the 'Paint-in' created a vast co-operative mural.

As well as publicising playgroups and PPA, branches were to hasten the development of playgroup courses, making representations to local colleges and adult education departments, and encouraging parents to take their first steps into what was for many a great new adventure: learning more about children, their needs and development.

By setting up bulk-buying schemes, branches also provided a vitally helpful service to playgroups: purchasing, storing and selling on paint, paper and other equipment to local groups. Greater activity at local level gave more parents opportunities to get involved in the movement, try their hand at new tasks, discover new capabilities and hone their skills, extending even further the web of friendship and mutual support.

Meetings were another forum for acquiring know-how, as well as stimulation, support and a recharging of batteries. At first, playgroup people went to meetings run by other organisations, especially meetings of the Nursery Schools Association. Wherever there were nursery schools or classes, or early years specialists in university departments or colleges, or such specialists who were retired, they were approached for advice and help.

A lecturer in Bradford described what happened to her:

> Before I could really give time and thought necessary to understand what the movement was about, a small group of young mothers came to see me at the college. To my surprise I found that already a number of playgroups were being formed in church halls, social clubs and community centres. As a trained and experienced pre-school educator I wondered how on earth they could expect to run a playgroup, provide the right kind of play materials and organise a good learning situation for the children without any training other than that of motherhood. But such was their tremendous enthusiasm that the whole idea caught on fast and when I went to an inspiring talk from the Pre-school Playgroups Association's first national adviser, I was won over completely and my concern was all for how best I could help and encourage this self-help movement. (Jessie Vaughan, 1981)

Not all early years professionals were as enthusiastic as this, and as PPA members' excitement grew at the success of what they were doing their enthusiasm may well have been exasperating to some nursery teachers who had spent many years fighting their corner within the educational establishment. Nevertheless, in almost every area teachers and lecturers gave time to help where they felt they could by writing, speaking at meetings, visiting playgroups and inviting playgroup people to visit their own settings.

Such expertise was especially welcome when PPA people sought good speakers as they began to get together at branch and county level to organise local conferences. These events, like PPA's famous national conferences, were run entirely by local volunteers. They provided invaluable opportunities for playgroup members to get together to compare ideas, share experiences, celebrate what they had achieved so far and enjoy one another's company while learning more about the needs of families and children and the ways these could be met in playgroup situations.

PPA at national level

Until 1966 most members of the PPA national executive committee, the NEC, had been drawn from the home counties. As the membership grew nationally, members from further afield joined the NEC. This, together with an office base and a part-time worker, brought about a feeling of progress and change.

The first office base was at Toynbee Hall, a former tenement block in the East End of London. There was no phone because it would have rung all day and the one person employed there would have been unable to tackle the rest of the work. The small room up several flights of outside steps had been painted by Enfield Branch – a gesture of appreciation and support for the national organisation from a nearby local one – and there was a bright red geranium on the windowsill outside. People still remember the red geranium – a symbol of triumph over adversity, providing cheerful reassurance that good things were happening here. Making the best of unsuitable premises was, after all, just part of the day's work for PPA at all levels!

This was indeed progress. Testimony in *Contact* from the NEC Secretary told members how things had been:

> How many of you, for instance, are aware that our last address (one of six we have already had since 1961) was only a forwarding one, and the bulk of our correspondence was being gallantly coped with by our previous secretary in her small back room – sans standard typewriter, filing cabinet, and all those essentials which ensure the smooth running of an office? It is quite impossible to convey to anyone the volume of work with which we are expected to cope, and the only way to appreciate this is to actually experience it in one's own home – and then vow most earnestly that this must never happen again! (*Contact*, October 1966)

The rescue money for administration had come from a small grant from the Nuffield Foundation. There was now a permanent address, but the pressure on the small central office workforce remained huge for years, their tolerance and good humour contributing enormously to the organisation's growing reputation and its continuing camaraderie.

PPA was to move again, twice, during these formative years: first to Borough High Street, near London Bridge, to rooms above the coal yard of Guy's

Hospital, and then to Alford House, in Kennington, near the Oval Cricket Ground. Here there were better conditions all round for a while, with some storage space and enough room to hold meetings, a luxury the organisation had been without for a long time. Until then regular meeting places had been in various parts of London, often near Euston and Kings Cross stations, where out-of-town members of the national committee caught trains home, sometimes late on Saturday evenings when trains were often full of rowdy football fans. Trains featured large in the lives of National Executive members. There were frequently discussions on trains, and always there were papers to read in advance on the way, or drafted on the way home, ready to be rapidly mailed.

Almost all paperwork was handwritten. Handwriting was recognised instantly, sometimes with pleasure, sometimes nervously. Most of those involved at all levels did more reading and writing and certainly more travelling than they had ever done, more talking and even perhaps more thinking.

NEC agendas were long. Committee meetings lasted all day, reflecting the inexperience of many of those participating, not least that of the chairman. Members took responsibility for different areas of work, and were relied on to do their homework and contribute reliably. Without exception they were able and committed, grounded in playgroup work in their own areas, with the confidence to help keep the committee's feet firmly on the ground. A little idealism was undoubtedly required but in the main what counted was practical knowledge of what was happening on the ground and what support was needed from the centre.

It was sometimes difficult to reach agreement on issues that were urgent and important. Elected members to the NEC were influenced, of course, by knowledge and experience of the playgroups in their own area, but conditions varied enormously, except that pressure, need and urgency existed everywhere. Some issues were difficult to resolve and raised strong feelings:

☐ Working out a way of structuring the organisation was important, but many members railed against consultation about how this new, young organisation was to be organised, feeling that it was trying to run before it could walk. This was perhaps the case, but grouping branches into counties within a regional framework, which is what was eventually agreed, paid off in the long run, when a few years later a very substantial grant for training and development across the country came from the government.

☐ Controversies over membership caused difficulty for a long time. Members sometimes assumed that joining a local branch made them members of the national organisation and complained when they did not receive *Contact*, which went monthly to people who paid the national membership subscription. There was disagreement also about whether individual membership should be distinguished from group membership. Having only groups as members would have made it much more straightforward to quantify numbers and be clear about distribution, but there were and had always been individual members, valued and contributing at all levels. Membership arrangements that distinguished between committee-run, parent-involving groups and others would also have simplified statistics, but PPA favoured a broad church approach, wanting to spread its influence as widely as possible.

☐ Fundraising raised issues too. As numbers grew nationwide, it became easier to attract commercial advertising, and care had to be taken to ensure that advertising was in line with the ethos of the movement.

☐ PPA had rapidly become a movement, and enthusiasm for all that was being achieved was growing rapidly too. Those working in playgroups were clamouring for courses to learn more, and arguments were developing both within and without PPA about the need for qualified staff and whether PPA should develop nationally recognised qualifications.

One of the factors that helped the growing movement resolve some of its issues, or at least to look at them from a fresh perspective, was a grant from the Department of Education in 1967, making it possible for a national adviser to tour the country. Her observations brought new insights and a more thoughtful assurance to PPA, enabling members to focus on what really mattered. About parent involvement she wrote at one point:

> I have known co-operative hall playgroups that involve mothers in only the most superficial way: the parents turn up, wash up, tidy up, and go home. Other groups may be private, with neither a rota nor a committee, and yet involve parents profoundly. (Crowe, 1973)

A new issue now began to be discussed: should playgroups still be thought of as a short-term expediency, or should they now be supported as an alternative provision for young families, valuable in their own right?

Meanwhile, campaigning continued. There were now playgroups in every constituency and it was possible to make sure that local MPs were kept informed about progress and concerns in order to maximise pressure in the House of Commons.

Breakthrough

Since its beginning PPA had been dismissed by some critics as being merely middle class, and as catering in its playgroups only for the children who least needed nursery provision. It has to be said that criticism of this kind frequently came from sources where little attempt had been made to check its accuracy. Pressure of work in PPA accelerated in the 1970s as Urban Aid (allocations of funding from central government to areas of special need) increased provision for under-fives, and more playgroup advisers were appointed by local authorities. Experienced area organisers who had worked as PPA volunteers for some years began to be appointed to these posts, linking new groups into the PPA network of support, and ensuring the active participation of parents. The view that playgroups could succeed only in middle-class neighbourhoods no longer held good, if indeed it ever had.

By this time not only did PPA have friends in Parliament, but there were influential supporters in other fields too. Eminent researchers and educationists, such as PPA's President Dr Wall, Willem van der Eyken, Penelope Leach, Dame Eileen Younghusband, Mia Kellmer Pringle, Lady Plowden – who was to become a very active and committed President – and others were publicly supporting PPA.

PPA officers were invited to the office of the Secretary of State for Social Services to discuss the speech that has become famously known as the Cycle of Deprivation speech. Sir Keith Joseph had chosen to deliver it as a major policy statement on provision for under-fives while opening the conference organised by PPA for local authority representatives in 1972. He also announced a huge increase in the PPA government grant, to provide regional offices and regional development officers. The letter confirming the grant said, 'We wish to see playgroups expanding, particularly in the priority areas of social deprivation' (*Contact*, July 1972).

Tyrrell Burgess had written in *Home and School* (1976):

> Since the most powerful influence on a child's early life is the home, can we plausibly seek to mitigate disadvantage by providing nursery schools? Should we not be seeking ways of operating directly on the home? The playgroup movement, whatever its weaknesses, offers a way of doing this which has eluded the school system as a whole ... helping the home through involving mothers and fathers in providing for the play needs of their own children.

By this time those who had reached an understanding of the value of parent participation in community provision for under-fives needed PPA to state its aims more clearly. It seemed now possible and expedient to redefine the aims. Working towards this, the National Executive in 1972 made the following statement:

> PPA exists to help parents to understand and provide for the needs of their young children. It aims to promote community situations in which parents can with growing enjoyment and confidence make the best uses of their own knowledge and resources in the development of their children and themselves.

Our hope was that this would enable the organisation to move forward with a more coherent purpose. The next chapter shows some of the ways these principles were embodied in playgroup provision for children and families.

2

The significance of play for children and parents

Linnet McMahon

> It is in playing and only in playing that the individual child is able to be creative and to use the whole personality, and it is only in being creative that the individual discovers the self. (Winnicott, 1971:54)

In the early days of the playgroup movement we understood something of the significance of play for children's development but there were gaps in our knowledge. In subsequent years a growing body of theory and research validated our intuitive understanding that play in its widest sense is vital in enabling people to be creative and autonomous. We now know too that the capacity to play develops where there is an emotionally containing and facilitating environment. If we can understand the relationship-based processes involved in establishing a facilitating environment we may be clearer about how to encourage the playful thinking and doing which is at the heart of being creative and autonomous children and adults. And society, having reached a nadir of mechanistic and bureaucratic box ticking, may now be at a point where creativity and self-direction can begin to be valued again.

Young mothers together setting up a playgroup – a personal experience

The most significant way in which we all learn is from personal experience. I start this chapter with an account of my own experience of starting a playgroup in the 1960s. I had returned from a few years abroad to spend a lonely and miserable winter, pregnant and with a toddler, in a rented upstairs flat with no stairgate. I was relieved and delighted to move to a village and a new housing estate where other young families were arriving. Our children met as they rode their tricycles round the block and so we mothers got to know one another. Like many mothers we were not working, expecting to be at home with our young children, often an isolating experience if you had moved away from family and friends. Hannah Gavron's *The Captive Wife* was widely read among *Guardian* readers like me and I had written a thesis on role conflict in young mothers! As elsewhere, there was no organised provision for young families in the village apart from the baby clinic. The state nursery school was in the town ten miles away and, even had it been able to offer a place, few mothers had regular use of a car. Long-standing village families relied on members of the extended family for help with children.

My neighbour was a Froebel teacher and I had some training in early childhood education. We had no thought for (or possibility of) going back to work and decided we would start a playgroup. We were absorbed by our children's development, but we felt that as our children reached the age of three they (and we) needed broader experience of the world than the home and immediate neighbourhood. Although, compared with today, children were still relatively free to play outside, this was happening less as people became more anxious about their children's safety. On the other hand we had no wish to leave our children with strangers; we wanted to be with them and to have new experiences together. We put up a notice in the village inviting people to join us, and gathered a wide range of women, from mothers like us with no local family to others who had grown up in the village, many of whom had left school at the earliest opportunity. Together we set up the playgroup in the village hall, taking turns minding each others' babies while the others ran the playgroup session. Grudgingly giving permission to use the hall, the village aristocracy warned, 'It will never last.' It is still going as I write, although the form it takes has undoubtedly changed.

All over the country there were other versions of this experience.

Children and mothers playing

What we were passionate about was spontaneous play, allowing children to choose what they did, within the safe framework of the playgroup session. We wanted to encourage exploration and creativity, imaginative and pretend play, in the company of other children. We saw playgroup as complementary to the close parent-child relationship at home, with its opportunities for conversation and more individual play, although we came to realise that not all children experienced this.

In the early days we had little money for equipment so we needed to be inventive and creative. We had plentiful supplies of used computer paper for drawing and painting. My husband made six small double-sided easels and we had jam jars of powder paint with huge brushes; washing lines across the hall were hung with glorious paintings. We saved household junk for sticking and making. We found planks and boxes for climbing. We went to the junk-yard for home corner stuff, painting old spoons and saucepans, finding camp beds and old screens for playing hospitals and zoos. We had tin trays and baby baths for sand and water play. We raided jumble sales for dressing-up clothes and hats. We made playdough. A father retrieved railway sleepers to make a much used woodwork bench.

Who was playing, you might ask. Certainly we were. We were thoroughly enjoying ourselves. We understood that one object could become another or be used or moved in a different way. What we were doing the children could do too. So we were happy to encourage children to be similarly inventive and creative. We provided the materials. They chose how they played with them.

The rationale for spontaneous, child-directed play

Where did this idea of spontaneous child-led play come from? The nursery schools that initially were our model made child-directed play the core of their practice. Influential nursery teacher Vera Roberts was clear that, 'The emphasis is on the provision of a rich play environment, with freedom for each child to choose his own activity and to continue with it as long as he wishes,' an environment in which, 'children should be given open-ended creative experience; that is to say, they should have the opportunity to use materials in new ways, to experiment, to explore possibilities, to take pleasure in the doing rather than in the end product,' adding tartly, 'There is no place in the nursery school for a detailed demonstration of, for example, how to make a piggy-bank from an empty squeezy bottle' (Roberts, 1971:6 and 20). Nursery teacher and lecturer Joan Cass was at pains to explain that the then current idea of permissiveness, often derided as 'let it all hang out' 1960s hippy culture, or feared as a selfish and combative free-for-all, was instead about children being:

> given permission to work at their own rate, and in their own time, and to choose how they work. This makes the whole process of learning interesting and exciting and children very soon meet the discipline that any activity in work or play sets them because of its own nature and purpose (Cass, 1971:145).

The Pre-school Playgroups Association's first national adviser Brenda Crowe, herself a Froebel nursery teacher, describes the similar 'freedom with responsibility', the security to explore within safe boundaries, that children experience in a good playgroup:

> In a happy, busy atmosphere children are painting, experimenting with wet and dry sand, water, clay, dough, bricks, woodwork, climbing apparatus and a wide variety of table-top toys; playing imaginatively in the home corner, or on improvised ships and buses; listening to stories; looking at books; enjoying music; singing; or chatting with interested adults about anything and everything. There will be ample opportunity for the children to respond to beauty in many forms; they will be stimulated to curiosity, wonder, reflection, discovery and the excitement of discovering, thinking, planning. There will be the security that comes from community rules kept out of consideration for others, and in this security the children will know freedom-with-responsibility. In this sort of atmosphere the children will truly feel 'free', and will be unaware that only subtle, unobtrusive control can give them this quality of freedom in which they can feel fearlessly happy and grow towards full stature. (Crowe, 1969)

The value of spontaneous play had been recognised even earlier. Psychoanalyst and educator Susan Isaacs had advised parents:

> It is a wise general rule to leave the children free to use their playthings in their own way – even if this does not happen to be the way that we might think the best. For play has the greatest value for the young child when it is really free and his own. (Isaacs, 1929:133)

She argued, too, that as well as playing at home young children need the company of other children:

> For some part of every day, young children ... should enjoy a time of free play with other children, not very much older or younger ... and if no nursery school is at hand, we must find ways of joining in with other parents to ensure that their children come together for free play as often as possible ... as free from grown-up interference as possible ... but within the real limits of physical safety.' (Isaacs, 1929:123)

She might have been making the case for parent-run playgroups long before they were dreamed of.

For many years Susan Isaacs was head of the Department of Child Development at London University, with enormous influence on the development of nursery education. Her psychoanalytic practice gave her insight into children's social and emotional needs which educational psychology had 'so piti-fully neglected'. Isaacs 'could show us the whole child, functioning as a whole, and she stopped us from thinking of learning as the sole business of the school, while emotion is relegated to the home or the clinic' (Gardner, 1969: 151). Isaacs was at pains to make clear that play and learning can only take place where the child feels both physically and emotionally safe. Harsh discipline constitutes a realisation of a child's 'phantastic dreads' while absence of support leaves them with deep anxiety about controlling their aggressive impulses. If a child is instead 'slowly educated by a tempered, real control, mild and understanding and appropriate to each situation as it arises' they are 'led forward on the path of real achievement' (Isaacs, in Gardner, 1969: 164). This emotional holding, 'mild and tempered, although firm and secure', enables children to manage their own anxious and angry feelings in the real world.

Although Isaacs' ideas influenced nursery education, they reached few post-war parents. Behaviourism and behaviour modification (based on Pavlov's dogs and Skinner's ideas on conditioned responses – its current version is cognitive behavioural treatment) held sway in psychology generally. Rigid baby and child training methods dominated advice to parents. The more flexible approach of Dr Spock brought relief to many parents in the 1960s. Later, Penelope Leach (1977) helped parents understand how a child's mind develops, and how the mother-child relationship can be a mutually satisfying process of growth. Meanwhile, nursery and infant schools, and in their turn playgroups, held onto the notion of developing the whole child through exploration and play.

Children and mothers playing and learning in playgroups
Many nursery teachers saw little place for mothers in the nursery school, other than settling in their children and receiving advice and support. While they recognised the significance of the mother-child relationship in children's emotional and intellectual development, they thought that by nursery school age the experts should complement and sometimes make up for the child's experience at home. This notion, with its 'deficit model' of the parental role, was widespread. Rare was someone like Margaret McMillan, an early pioneer of nursery education in a poor area of east London, who considered that the nursery school should be an 'efficient and homelike' extension of family life, a place where mothers might have their own contribution to make. She saw 'no reason at all why ... it should not one day be presided over by the mothers themselves' (McMillan, 1919).

The quality of play provision in playgroups could – and did – vary. The model advocated by the Pre-school Playgroups Association was that of a good nursery school, but it was then left to the groups themselves to negotiate 'the intricacies of the extra dimension occasioned by parent involvement' (Crowe, 1973:62). In the absence of a theory that would embrace both, this sometimes entailed a real conflict of ideology. It needed huge skill to keep in mind both the needs of children for good play provision and also the desire to ensure that all mothers, whatever their ideas about what children should be doing in the playgroup, not only felt welcome and at home but also shared the responsibility for the playgroup. Many of the mothers setting up playgroups were well educated and open to ideas about developing the whole child and learning through play. In sympathy with the rise of feminist ideas, they enjoyed the creativity and autonomy of starting a playgroup, with benefits for themselves and their children. Other mothers were from a generation whose schooling had been more about 'filling empty vessels' than 'lighting a fire'. National adviser Brenda Crowe tried to explain to this group that:

> playgroup leaders defeat the very thing they are trying to bring about if they teach children to 'make things' before the children have had hours and hours of individual exploration in order to discover some of the properties of paper, paint, glue, clay, dough and wood, as 'stuff'. Similarly, children are robbed of the chance to learn to make decisions for themselves if they are endlessly required to be pliable and responsive to orders (*op cit*, 64).

Standard of play provision, or value of a group in a particular community?

Yet Brenda Crowe was wary of dismissing a group as inadequate without first considering the value of a playgroup in its particular community. The question should be about what is happening in the playgroup and in the homes of these children. If the children are having a greater range of stimulating experience and the mothers are happier and less anxious, she said, then it is a good playgroup. Here are two examples, the first from then Pre-school Playgroups Association (PPA) training and development officer Jill Faux and the second from project co-ordinator Shirley Palfreeman:

> I remember visiting a group in an Educational Priority Area and being asked by the play leader to sit at a table with a mother and some children playing with Constructo-straws. She told me the mother was inclined to drink too much and was lacking in confidence and self-esteem. I started to put some straws together as I talked to her and the children. After a while I pushed some straws towards her and said, 'Come on, have a go.' She looked at me in panic and

said, 'I don't know how to do it.' She thought I was constructing something pre-determined and knew precisely what straw would fit next. I pulled my totally irre-levant creation apart and starting again we took it in turns to add another straw to an ever growing contraption. The children joined in, and in no time at all she was laughing and actively playing. It impressed me because it was the first time I had met someone so insecure she could do nothing for herself. In a way we had to reinvent the wheel in order to own it. Doing it with mothers, having fun, watching the light dawn over and over again, was what was so exhilarating.

A playgroup we helped to establish in a run-down area of town seemed to be going well. Two play leaders had been on playgroup courses and appeared to be well organised and involving the mothers; everyone seemed happy. When I called in early one morning the noise could be heard from far off. Inside the chil-dren were tearing round on bikes or running round shouting and swinging on the altar rails (the group was in a community church). Both play leaders were off sick and the mothers were organising the group, with no sign of the carefully chosen activities, painting, water play or books. Children and mothers looked happy and pleased, explaining that the children needed to 'let off steam' before settling down for their 'schooling'. Thirty minutes later out came the other activi-ties. The mothers had decided that this was the best way to organise the group, and they were right. Most of the families lived in flats and the children had little chance to be physically active.

The benefits to the mother-child relationship could be great. In some de-prived communities, especially designated Educational Priority Areas, people were encouraged to work with mothers and children together in community projects (an early version of family centres and children's centres). There was evidence to support such work. One of the long-term outcomes of the Head-start pre-school programme in the United States was that where parents were involved, children grew up achieving significantly more in education and em-ployment (Consortium for Longitudinal Studies, 1979).

The notion that the value of a playgroup to a particular community was a better criterion than a general standard of play provision led to fierce debate within the playgroup movement, and was the point at which some people left. Undoubtedly there were playgroups, whether in well-off or poorer areas, with poor provision for children's play and learning and where mothers had limited opportunities for playing and learning themselves. The hope was that their inclusion within the Pre-school Playgroups Association left the door open to change; sometimes this happened, sometimes not. Even so, many playgroups offered mothers new opportunities for friendship, for playing and learning, changing their view of themselves and their children, with long-term benefits for their children's self-esteem as well as their educational future.

Children playing and learning – a national survey

The huge expansion nationwide of pre-school playgroups directly benefited thousands of children. By 1980 over half a million children, mainly three or four years old, attended the 15,000 playgroups in membership of the Pre-school Playgroups Association. Children enjoyed playing together and made friends, often across social class and ethnic group. A national survey described the views of 459 mothers in 32 playgroups held in halls – home playgroups were not included (Gray and McMahon, 1982). Mothers recognised the value of play and the opportunities for play that a playgroup can provide. They particularly valued the social benefits for their children. Nine out of ten mothers said that playgroup made their children more confident without them, and better at playing with other children; they were learning more and were generally happier. They said:

> It's a chance to mix with other children.
>
> She's more confident and independent, less shy.
>
> They have new activities not provided at home – sand, the slide, music and singing.

Many added that their children were more interesting and easier to get on with: 'It's something for us to talk about.' There were possible losses if children were cooped up in village and church halls rather than playing in neighbourhoods, or if play provision was spectacularly boring and constrained – 'They tend to put the same things out each week' – but most children attended only two or three half-days a week, leaving opportunity for other experiences. The picture changed a little as children became rising-five, with mothers commenting, 'As children got older I should have liked to have seen more imaginative opportunities for play activities,' or asking for formal teaching: 'I think the children should learn their numbers and letters.' Some local publications – *Serendipity* (Scottish PPA), *Rising Five* (Oxfordshire PPA and Education Dept), *See the Daisies, Feel the Rain* (Greater London PPA) – addressed this issue.

Benefits to the mother-child relationship

What was clear from the survey was that:

> A playgroup forms a bridge for the mother and young child between their life at home and the world outside, at a stage when the child needs the stimulation of

new faces and new activities. Their relationship takes on a new dimension as their horizons are broadened by the experiences and people they meet at the playgroup, and by their growing independence. (Gray and McMahon:5)

More than eight out of ten mothers in the study said that playgroup helped them understand how children learn through play. 'It has developed in her things that I didn't think could be developed in a child of that age.' Many mothers worried about how they were bringing up their children and said that it helped to see what other children were like and to hear that other mothers had the same problems. More than six in ten mothers said that playgroup helped them get on better with their children, saying, for example:

> I understand her more.
>
> It has made me more confident in the upbringing of my children.
>
> I feel part of my child's learning process.
>
> I think others sometimes think of it as a substitute for school which is quite wrong in my view.

They valued having a break from their child, giving them some breathing space, 'just to be 'me' for a little while', or more time to spend with a baby, while confident their child was with people they trusted; mother and child appreciated each other the more as a result. Often the whole family benefited as relationships eased.

The mothers in this survey were not just from the middle classes. Nearly half their partners had manual jobs, and a few were unemployed. Most fathers were involved in bringing up their children, sometimes in the playgroup. In any case they generally approved of playgroup and tolerated its demands on mothers' time. More than one in four mothers also had paid work, usually part-time and outside playgroup hours. In 3 per cent of families English was not the first language.

Mothers playing and learning

In the early years of the playgroup movement we didn't need to think about parent involvement because we were the parents. Involvement was about having a sense of ownership and autonomy; it was not about joining or running a playgroup on someone else's terms.

For most mothers playgroups had an important social function; it was somewhere to meet people and make friends. Depression was a significant problem for isolated mothers cooped up at home. Some playgroups were better than others in understanding mothers' underlying anxiety, feelings of inadequacy and loss of identity. Many playgroups were welcoming, involving places, and mothers valued feeling that they had something to contribute. Three in four mothers in the survey said that taking part in running their playgroup was rewarding and that playgroup made them happier (Gray and McMahon, 1982). Mothers who felt valued grew in self-confidence and so became more able to take the emotional risk of opening their minds to new ideas.

However, it was in the most fully involving parent-run playgroups, where parents both shared the responsibility for managing the group and also took an active part in playgroup sessions, that mothers said they gained most confidence in themselves as mothers and individuals. These women felt that playgroup had helped them understand their children better and put more emphasis than others on the fact that their children were happier. They welcomed the stimulation of new play activities and friends for their children, as they did for themselves, and made less mention of formal schooling. This raised an important question:

> Do these playgroups, by expecting and enabling parents to share responsibility, lead mothers to expect their own children to benefit from and enjoy similar situations of sharing and learning? As mothers gain in confidence themselves, they may also grow in confidence in their children's ability to learn and grow (*op cit*, 59).

Through working and playing together playgroup mothers were developing their own skills: in management, negotiation, diplomacy, advocacy, leadership, nurturing and enabling, often transcending class and culture barriers and addressing the sidelining of women in society. They were excited to find they were capable of more than they had ever imagined. Their sense of self, of personal autonomy, grew as their role and standing outside the family developed. This could change the balance of roles and power within the family, affecting husband-wife relationships – for better or worse. Perhaps there were times too when a mother's growth was at the expense of the child's good experience – 'Mummy's at *another* meeting.'

Yet children also benefited from seeing that their mothers were active, able adults outside the home, playing an important role in the community – a good role model. The mothers in the groups were volunteers, in that payment was minimal or non-existent, but, more importantly, they were members. What mothers were doing was, like their children, learning through play, in the sense that they were able to try things out – or try new ways of being – in an emotionally facilitating environment where it felt safe, where it was all right to make mistakes. In the process they created something new, or became someone different. They were developing a sense of autonomy and identity, which meant that they in turn could help their children to become thinking, self-directing, autonomous members of society.

Experiential learning as the foundation for practice – strengths and weaknesses

The Pre-school Playgroups Association took a practical approach in its publications and on its courses. The playgroup magazine *Contact* provided a welcome mix of stimulating ideas and reassurance. Playgroup advisers and tutors (Crowe, 1969; Jarecki, 1975; Lucas and Henderson, 1981) produced influential publications, all packed with invaluable advice on setting up and running a playgroup, what material to provide for play, how to provide safe boundaries and how to respond to children whose behaviour was difficult or who had special needs. However, the tone was personal, sympathetic and sensitive, aware that mothers and playgroup leaders were doing their best for their children based on their previous experience:

> An established playgroup does not always need 'more things to do'; still less does it need 'more things to make'. The real need is for greater awareness in ourselves. We need ... to know when to use a natural opportunity to discuss something with the children; to know how to encourage them to think for themselves ... Playgroups aren't just about children. They are also about us and our relationships, both with children and each other. (Crowe, 1969:55)

Much thought was given to parents' feelings and needs.

Experiential learning – memories, child observation and workshops

Playgroup courses drew on adult learning principles, fundamentally that effective learning was experiential (Rogers, 1971). Often the starting point in understanding the value of play was to recall memories of our own childhood play, as a member of a tutors' course describes:

> Brenda asked us what we had valued as play as children, what we remembered ... One member remembered washing dolls' clothes in a butt in the garden: the soapflakes squashed together under water; the dripping clothes; winding the mangle; squeezing out the water; and the fights that arose with the many other children who came to the garden. She can still feel in memory the joy of water. Another spoke of scrubbing her grandfather's white collars; the smoothness of the soap on the collar; the patterns of the scrubbing brush; the corrugations on the wooden draining board; scraping the water off the board; the feel of the bristles on the brush; the cold jellyness of water-saturated soap.

Observing children was another key to understanding a child's whole experience. Susan Isaacs had emphasised the need to watch children play rather than pontificate about theory:

> By watching our children play we gain a fuller knowledge of children in general, and of our own children in particular. And without that knowledge how shall we guide them? (Isaacs, 1929:123)

In playgroup courses, often informal *Playing, Living and Learning* doorstep courses, a series of meetings at the playgroup, first-hand observation of children was ideally suited to mothers' learning, matching their learning though experience in the playgroup. For those fearful about their own academic abilities, to be asked 'Would you spend five minutes watching children at the dough table and just jot down what you notice?' was minimally threatening.

As ever there were mothers anxious that their children should be ready for school, perhaps to have a happier and more successful experience of education than they themselves had had. They wanted children to be taught, numbers and colours for instance, and feared that play was not enough. Only by seeing for themselves that children learn through play could they start to relinquish deep-held convictions. As they themselves played in workshops with materials such as sand and water, dough, clay and paint, they experienced the joy (and fears) of exploring, experimenting, being destructive and being creative. They could try out ideas without fear of failure because the process was what mattered, not an end product.

Absence of any theory that embraced both play and the mother-child relationship

The emphasis in playgroup courses on experiential learning meant that real learning took place, rather than an arid acquisition of theory that had little impact on practice. However, there was a drawback. The lack of an overall theory, backed by research, meant that it was not easy to make a good case to the outside world for children's need for spontaneous play or for the benefits of parental involvement and responsibility. Neither was nursery training able to offer research-backed validation for these benefits to children and adults.

Courses gave attention to stages of development, and of intellectual development in particular, influenced by the ideas of Piaget (1926/1959). Piaget was interested in how children develop language and thinking, and he was also aware of the therapeutic benefits of imaginative play in helping children master fears and phantasies. He maintained a welcome emphasis on play which he saw as the child's way of assimilating, making sense of, internalising their experience – making it part of themselves; the complementary process was accommodation as the child learned to meet the demands of the real world.

Attachment theory was in its infancy, with much antipathy to Bowlby, who was seen as holding back mothers' own development by tying them to the home. There was little understanding of different kinds of mother-child attachment and the dynamics of these relationships, which would have helped make sense of them. Neither nursery nor playgroup courses covered psychoanalytic ideas about unconscious mental processes, although this would have been invaluable in understanding projected feelings – that the way other people made you feel was a useful indicator of how they themselves were really feeling (McMahon and Ward, 2001). It would have helped make sense of personal attacks and hostility, limiting the personal hurt people felt and allowing them to respond to the underlying feeling – for example, to the fear that is often behind anger. Isaacs' profound understanding of the development of the child's inner world of thoughts and feelings, based on the child's first relationships with the mother or other significant person at home, was lost, along with her awareness of the unconscious processes underlying emotional containment, except in the simplest sense.

Theory of emotional development risked being watered down into a recital of Erikson's (1965) developmental tasks of achieving basic trust, autonomy and initiative. Vital though understanding these stages is, there was less insight into what the child's inner world was like when these tasks were not achieved – the implications for a child (and adult) whose expectations of the world were of mistrust, shame, doubt and guilt. There was some good advice on managing behaviour in general but less insight about how to help a mother-child relationship in difficulty, although of course there were people who offered invaluable help and support to some mothers. Winnicott's idea (1965) of emotional holding and the facilitating environment – both why it matters and how to provide it – scarcely reached us.

The exception was awareness of the meaning of separation for the child, as Bowlby's (1965) ideas on attachment and separation gained wider currency, largely through the powerful films (the first in 1953) of James and Joyce Robertson, who filmed the increasing distress of young children separated from their mothers without the provision of a substitute attachment figure, and the corollary – how distress could be minimised by an emotionally containing mother substitute. The result was careful attention to the process of settling children into playgroup or nursery.

Demands for more rigour in education

Child-centred practice in playgroups was underpinned by the Plowden Report (1967), which had argued that a technological society needed flexible and creative thinkers, to be produced by schools with a more play-based curriculum tailored to the needs and interests of the child. While the transmission model probably remained dominant, a more relaxed approach meant that children enjoyed primary school. Doubts crept in with anxiety that children from more disadvantaged families and communities had inadequate language and communication skills (Bernstein, 1971). Government demanded more rigour in primary education. Infant schools started to introduce the structured language and play programmes advocated by Joan Tough (1974) and others. The culture of structuring play seeped down into nursery classes in schools (by the late 1970s more numerous than separate nursery schools) and into playgroups. Nursery educator Joan Cass warned:

> It seems a little unfortunate that in some quarters today there is a certain reaction against children's spontaneous play, which it is felt so often to be more usefully directed by the skilled adult into carefully planned learning experiences. Of course children want to learn and the adult must provide a challenging and stimulating environment in which optimum learning can take place. Great care, however, is needed, for structures disguised as play can sometimes be unimaginative, uninspired and adult-oriented and hinder development rather than help it. (Cass, 1975:20)

This timely warning went largely unheeded. At best people using these programmes in playgroups were attuned to the responses of individual children. At worst it was a didactic parody (Maxwell, 1984) of what they thought nursery teaching was – doing 'floating and sinking' *ad nauseam*. Later studies, such as Barbara Tizard's (1984), demonstrated that the apparent deficiencies of disadvantaged children were largely a myth (children and parents at home had elaborate shared conversations) and were more a consequence of the social structures of class, power and prejudice that the children encountered outside the home. But the damage had been done.

The basis for cognitive development in human interaction – Bruner's research into early years practice

A major research study of children's experience in different forms of early years provision in England was led by respected American psychologist Jerome Bruner, who had taken Piaget's ideas a stage further to show that cognitive development had its basis in human interaction. Bruner (1985:32) wrote:

> The world is a symbolic world in the sense that it consists of conceptually organised, rule bound belief systems about what exists, about how to get to goals, about what is to be valued. There is no way, none, in which a human being could possibly master that world without the aid and assistance of others for, in fact, that world is others.

This has resonance today with the prevailing idea that a child's experience is always culturally mediated, often through language, but also through how things are presented.

The detailed observations of the Oxford Pre-school Research Group showed that what helped develop children's concentration and thinking was the 'scaffolding' provided by stimulating adults. Play that developed in complexity was most likely when an adult was close by, when only two children were playing together, or when the setting was intimate – such as a cosy corner or den. Further, the observations revealed that most adult talk in playgroups, nursery schools and classes was about managing the group's activities or giving instructions. Rather little took the form of connected turn-taking contingent conversations with children, where each made a contribution and listened to one another. Yet it was in these conversations that children were developing their ability to think and reflect. Adults asking too many questions were discouraging, and adults asking questions to which they already knew the answer were a complete turn-off. The conclusion was that the role of the helpful adult was to provide a 'buffer to distraction' and to 'entice the children into more complex play' (Bruner, 1980:66). One way was to encourage conversations and stories about children's experiences of other times, places and people, rather than the here and now. Another was to provide a non-intrusive commentary on, or join in, play, especially pretend play, but contingent on the child's response.

Perhaps Bruner's most important contribution was to make clear that a child's development did not depend simply on the provision of the right materials or input. The capacity to think grows out of relationships, within and outside the home, where people listen to one another, talking and playing together. Here was the beginning of a more useful theory to explain what was happening in good playgroups. In later years when I became interested in play therapy I realised that the listening, reflective, commenting adult role Bruner advocated had much in common with a play therapist's attentive, reflective stance in enabling emotionally distressed or damaged children to heal themselves through play. Play therapy has its theory base in psychoanalytic ideas of emotional containment and the facilitating environment, a subject to which I will return.

Bruner realised that much research failed to influence practice:

> In the realm of child care when one is dealing with concerned people, new knowledge *about* children that comes from *outside* one's own experience seems to make little headway against received wisdom and 'commonsense' practice. It is only when the research helps one to see with one's own eyes that it gets beneath the skin. (Bruner, 1980:211)

Accordingly he recruited practitioners as researchers, including playgroup tutors of whom I was one. We modified the child observation method into one that became widely used on playgroup foundation courses (Holmes and McMahon, 1979). Its structured observations matched new demands for rigour, yet were consistent with earlier playgroup approaches to learning about child development through observing – it was the process of learning from one's own experience that had the power to change approaches and attitudes. In retrospect, I think the approach was too structured, even while it ensured that learning through child observation continued. It became one of the tools for professionalising playgroup courses, which was happening in the 1980s.

The decline of playfulness

Playgroup courses struggled to remain experiential and engaging, still giving opportunities for mothers to play and learn, in the face of coping with the introduction of a curriculum and eventually a qualification. In those years playgroups were becoming increasingly the province of playgroup leaders or supervisors, with parents limited to coming in on a rota and taking part in the management committee. The playfulness of mothers, and playgroup leaders, tended to be lost in a more bureaucratic and routinised approach to running a playgroup. Perhaps this was inevitable; the excitement and challenge of starting something new requires different skills from those needed to sustain an existing organisation. The outlook of keeping things going does not invite the creativity and exploration of play. As the adults became less playful this was transmitted to the children in the predictability and limitations of the play that was provided and encouraged.

Broader social changes were taking place. In the 1960s and 1970s Brenda Crowe had urged mothers to survive saying no to their children and stay in charge of toddler tantrums, but she was up against a generation of relatively deprived mothers who wanted to give their children what they themselves had never had, and who saw this in terms of material possessions and success rather than love and containment. Brenda Crowe warned in vain about the consequences and we reaped the whirlwind in Thatcher's children. Thatcherism was about the individual, not society; social values shifted in the direction of selfishness and greed. Marketisation and managerialism, with their tick-box targets, replaced professionalism and emotional containment in the workplace. This meant loss of the capacity to think and reflect. With the coming of the National Curriculum after 1988 teachers lost their autonomy to decide what was taught. Although they were supposed to retain how it was taught this too was undermined by prescription, testing and inspection. This mindset trickled down into playgroups, as they too lost much of their autonomy. These factors, together with the growth of a risk averse culture, led to diminished opportunities for children's spontaneous and creative play. Individualism also meant the loss of a sense of belonging to or playing a part in the community. In many ways this is still the prevailing culture, although there is an uneasy sense that something important has been lost.

Making the case for play – the need for theory and research

From Isaacs to Bruner, as well as in the playgroup movement, there was agreement that effective practice must be based on experiential learning, and that child development in particular was best learned through observing children. Equally, all had experienced the frustration of being unable to influence powerful policy makers who had little understanding of child development or who held different values and priorities. Managers and politicians (having neither time nor inclination) are not going to learn this experientially. They need some other way of understanding what children need: something scientific, such as outcome studies, and something that they can grasp quickly by reading – for preference on no more than one side of A4.

Like others before them, people in the Pre-school Playgroups Association could not supply this, other than in the notion, relatively new then but taken for granted now, that the child's experience in the early years is crucial to how they develop later. Even so, policy makers may have different notions of childhood, different values for learning and education, different priorities. Despite the lip service paid to evidence-based practice today, the evidence of research is rarely the major influence in choice of a policy; rather it is used where it supports an already chosen policy priority. However, it is usually the best resource we have got. (Having friends in high places is another!) People in the playgroup movement whose learning was, as we have seen, largely experiential had little firepower with which to challenge the policy makers who had the power to make a difference. What was needed, then and now, was a good body of theory, backed up by research, to provide the coherent argument for play.

The function of play

What is play? Children are often said to be just playing, as if what they are doing is unimportant. Yet play is a child's work. For children play is essential as a way of helping them make sense of the world and having some control over their lives. We can understand this when we think about our own needs as adults for play. Most of us are familiar with the mental freezing that goes with pressure. If someone is explaining how to use a new piece of technology we can feel increasingly muddled and anxious, longing for them to stop talking so that we can 'play' on our own and gradually become more familiar with this new thing. We may find that if we stop thinking about a particular problem, 'we may be surprised to find an answer popping unexpectedly into our heads: our mind has been left to play, quietly wandering round the problem, and has found a solution' (McMahon, 2009:6). It is the same for children. Making sense of the world is an enormous task but they are less able to find the words, and also have less autonomy, than adults. 'Play under the control of the player gives to the child his first and the most crucial opportunity to have the courage to think, to talk and perhaps even to *be* himself' (Bruner, 1983). In play a child can explore and create, find out how things and people work, and give the imagination free rein. Unlike adults who can mull things over in their minds, children need to re-enact events or play out strong feelings, in the process gaining a sense both of inner peace and of the world feeling more manageable.

Paediatrician and psychoanalyst Donald Winnicott argued that in play the child is connecting their inner world with some aspect of outside reality, which is the beginning of symbolisation and of creativity. For example, the growing child's separation anxiety is often helped by a soft toy, ribbon or blanket (their transitional object), which becomes the child's chosen comforter or friend. It is both a real object and one that has emotional meaning for the child, a symbolic means of managing anxiety and perhaps the child's first creation. This is a reminder of the crucial link between play and the development of a sense of identity, of being an individual: 'It is playing and only in playing that the individual child is able to be creative and to use the whole personality, and it is only in being creative that the individual discovers the self' (Winnicott, 1971).

Play is the key to development of the sense of self and of the ability to think, to connect thinking and feeling. This is the case for children but equally for adults, for mothers, for parents. How does this come about?

Emotional holding and the facilitating environment

The essentials for play to take place are:

- [ ] autonomy – the need for the player to feel in control of the play and the direction it takes, whether or not another person is present or playing
- [ ] no serious consequences – the process of playing matters more than the results: mistakes do not have serious consequences which means that risks can be taken
- [ ] safe boundaries – the need for the player to feel safe within a physical boundary of time and space, where the rules of everyday life do not apply, and to feel well-enough held emotionally, whether or not a 'containing' person is actually present. (McMahon, 2009:8)

Origins of the capacity to play in the holding environment

Winnicott argued that the beginning of play is in the safe space, the 'potential space', between a mother and her baby, where the mother 'makes ready what the baby is prepared to find.' The infant has the 'illusion of autonomy' and feels free to explore and play, and so is able to think and learn. The 'good enough' mother is attuned to the subtle cues as to how her baby is feeling, making a space in her mind where she digests this, sometimes consciously but often without being aware of doing so. Bion (1962) calls this process of being open to being stirred up emotionally 'maternal reverie'. The mother's task is to tolerate without being overwhelmed by her infant's feelings, and give back more loving than anxious or hating feelings. This enables the developing child to be able to bear the experience of having both loving and angry or fearful feelings about the same person. The child becomes able to hold onto and think about these mixed emotions, rather than simply to get rid of the uncomfortable feelings through some kind of physical expression or mental suppression. In other words, instead of being driven by anxiety about how to get good enough care, the child internalises the experience of being emotionally held and so develops a mind able to hold thoughts (Waddell, 2002).

A mother – or person in the mothering role; it might be a father – is able to provide emotional holding only if she too is emotionally held by those close to her, or by her past good experience. They in their turn need the emotional holding of a society that recognises the value of what they are doing. This is Winnicott's facilitating environment (*The Maturational Processes and the Facilitating Environment*, 1965), made up of concentric circles of emotional containment.

Attachment theory and research – secure attachment as the basis for play

Winnicott's idea of emotional holding and the facilitating environment is supported by the vast body of theory and research on attachment theory, further supported by growing neuro-physiological evidence. Attachment theory is about the development of the different forms of the child's attachment to the mother (or other attachment person). This attachment may be more or less secure. Secure attachment means that the child has a secure base (Bowlby's phrase), which frees the child to explore and find out about the world. This sense of a secure base being available is initially about the mother's physical and emotional holding in the first years of life. This does not mean being glued to the child 24 hours a day as Bowlby was initially interpreted but, as Winnicott and others showed, is more about the provision in the mother's mind of an inner mental space for the child. The child who feels reliably and predictably 'held in mind' feels secure and confident enough to explore, play and think. This experience becomes internalised so that the child develops an inner representational model of the world and of other people as trustworthy and loving and the self as worthy of that love.

There are degrees and kinds of a child's attachment, ranging from secure to anxious, arising out of different kinds of mother-child relationships (Crittenden, 2000). Understanding of these is a valuable tool in working out how to help both the child and the parent where there are difficulties. An anxiously attached child cannot play and think without some kind of emotional holding or containment. Parents of course have their own attachment (more or less secure) based on their past history. It affects their view of themselves and it affects their mothering and ability to provide emotional holding. If there are attachment difficulties, early intervention can make a difference to the future of child and mother.

The playgroup as a facilitating environment

A playgroup that supports the mother-child relationship can help to sustain or encourage a secure attachment, enabling the child to explore and play and be creative, as Winnicott explained. This is genuine independence, in which initial reliable dependence has given the child confidence that their dependency needs will be met when they arise, rather than the false independence of the anxious child having to cope too early on their own. Further, a playgroup can provide a secure base – Winnicott's holding or facilitating environment – for an anxiously attached mother (which was probably most of us, if in varying degrees) and so allow her too to explore, play and be creative. In the process the mother-child relationship is strengthened, and both gain emotionally and intellectually.

Perhaps the facilitating environment can be symbolised as a set of Russian dolls. The Pre-school Playgroups Association and the elements in society which supported a good playgroup provided the external containment for those whose task was to run the playgroup; they in turn provided the emotional holding for the playgroup mothers (and sometimes the fathers or other family members), enabling them to provide emotional holding for their child. The child needs the holding of both mother and the community of playgroup people, providing a safe potential space in which they can play and grow into thinking, feeling, autonomous and competent individuals.

Why the idea of play in a facilitating environment is relevant now
Two current voices:

> Children are not playing at life; it's more serious than that. They are working at how to live. (Psychoanalyst Adam Phillips, 2010)

> An education where you don't find out who you are is to my mind not an education. (Children's Laureate and poet, Michael Rosen, 2010)

Over thirty years ago Jerome Bruner wrote, with prescience:

> Economics, chilling and compelling though the immediate prospects may be, does not justify risking a generation ... The object of education at any age is surely broad and plural: to produce competent and zestful human beings who can manage their own lives and contribute to the common good while doing so. (Bruner, 1980:5 and 10)

Today this is echoed in Robin Alexander's Cambridge Primary Review (2009), which argues for an education that heeds children's voices and empowers them for life as both learners and citizens. He calls for a 'dialogic education', with a focus on talk that is 'reciprocal and cumulative' – a resonance with Bruner's 'turn-taking contingent conversation'. The Review deplores the decline of community and the massive inequality, with its tale of disadvantage, poverty and under-achievement, in England today and asks that childhood's rich potential should be protected from 'a system apparently bent on pressing children into a uniform mould at an ever-younger age.'

There are other moves to encourage play and creativity in the early years, mainly influenced by the Italian Reggio Emilia approach (Edwards *et al*, 1998), itself grounded in the community's political desire for its children to think for themselves. This approach views the child as competent and autonomous, able to make meaning from experience. The adult's role is to support the child's interests and encourage a creative and playful exploration of the physical and cultural world around them. Children are seen as the collective responsibility of a closely connected community, in which parents have a vital role in shaping services. In translation to a British context, such as the 5x5x5 project (Drummond, 2005; Bancroft *et al*, 2008), there has been surprise and delight, both in the flourishing of children's creative thinking and in the development of a community of adult relationships built on a spirit of enquiry, reflection and playful thinking. Adults have learned about their own capacities for growth and change. There has been astonishment at the high level of parental involvement! Here is another facilitating environment, with the possibility of exercise of democratic power in a local community. Such initiatives mean living with uncertainty and open-mindedness, and how well they will fare long term in a more competitive and highly regulated society is yet to be seen. It is worth trying. Certainly children's centres and family centres need understanding of the benefits of play in a facilitating environment – and how to provide it – if they are to further the development of happier and more competent children and families.

From the playgroup movement we can learn how to provide the space within which children and their families from all walks of life, sometimes together, sometimes in separate ways, have the potential to play, be creative, bring together thoughts and feelings, learn and think and reflect, and so develop a fuller sense of self and self-esteem. It is not only about children playing and learning but also about adults learning through playing. Ultimately, it is about using ourselves, which means using spontaneity, playfulness and self-awareness in engaging with others – children, parents and professionals – to nurture their development and competence. Creating and sustaining a facilitating environment, a community based on social co-operation, is difficult work. Those involved need their own holding environment, their own containing and reflective space within which they can play without fear with their thoughts and feelings. It may currently be the road less travelled, but it could make all the difference.

3

Learning on PPA courses

Sue Griffin

Courses are the keystone of the playgroup world. Courses enable mothers to understand what children in a playgroup need, and give them confidence eventually to run a playgroup themselves if they so wish. Furthermore, nearly all the students take away from the course more than playgroup expertise: they have an increased understanding of their own children and other adults, which goes with them for the rest of their lives. This is one of PPA's greatest contributions to the community. (Inner London Pre-school Playgroups Association 1976 in *Playgroups – a shared adventure*)

One of the greatest achievements of the Pre-school Playgroups Association (PPA) was the contribution it made not only to pre-school education but also to adult education, pioneering lifelong learning many years before that phrase became fashionable. From its earliest days, PPA was not just about children's development and learning but also about the personal development and learning of adults. It is significant that the key regional staff roles created from 1972 onwards were given the job title 'training and development officers' (TDOs), showing the priority attached to courses in the range of PPA activities.

PPA courses were mainly attended by women, for many of whom they represented a second chance to engage with learning and education in a way they found more comfortable and enjoyable than the first time round. They joined the courses to find out about children and playgroups, but gained much else, including self-esteem, self-confidence and skills in communicating with other adults.

45

Early courses grew from small informal groups of adults involved in play-groups, exchanging information and ideas. By the 1990s, a complex structure of basic and introductory courses, doorstep courses, the Foundation Course, specialist courses, fieldwork courses and tutor-training courses had developed, organised by PPA to meet the varying needs of playgroup people – play leaders and parents, as well as committee members, PPA staff and volunteers at all levels. But, whatever the course, however long or short, how-ever basic or advanced, PPA courses had a profound effect on many people's lives.

This chapter explores this effect, illuminating some of the principles that underpinned PPA, by looking at:

- ☐ **why** PPA courses emerged, why they were required, what their pur-pose was seen to be
- ☐ **who** participated in the courses, both course members and tutors
- ☐ **what** courses developed and **what** they were about – their content
- ☐ **where** and **when** they were run
- ☐ **how** they were organised and funded, and the teaching methods used.

The why, who, what, when, where and how of PPA courses all evolved and changed throughout the phases of PPA's development, in response both to what PPA volunteers and staff discovered about offering opportunities for adults to learn, and to the changes in the world of adult education and society at large. No description of PPA courses could characterise them all, and dur-ing the lifetime of PPA there was no blueprint for the perfect course handed down from on high. What follows offers examples of common or widespread practices, which emerged as creative and committed people throughout the organisation sought to meet the needs of learners who joined courses, and thus of the children and families in the playgroups.

It is difficult to indicate precise dates for the developments and changes des-cribed; they evolved at varying paces in different parts of the country, res-ponding, like other PPA developments, to local need. PPA's branch/county/ regional/national structure enabled information to be shared, so what had been successful in one area could be tried elsewhere, adapted and refined, if necessary, to fit a different local context.

Why?

Almost as soon as the first playgroups were established, parents realised that, if they were to sustain the responsibility of running their own groups, they had a lot to learn. They were pioneering every challenging step in creating a form of provision not seen in our society before. They needed to learn about children – how to provide play that would help children develop and enjoy learning, and how to respond to the way children behaved. They needed to learn about adults – how to get and keep parents involved in playgroups, and how to communicate and negotiate with professionals in the early years field and with purse-string holders. They needed to learn about organisation – how to run the business and administration side of a playgroup and how to work together in committees:

> The adults involved in playgroups needed and demanded help. They were after all doing something innovative and demanding. (Lee Fairlie, playgroup parent)

One example of the origins of courses is the playgroup pioneer in the1960s who began to hold meetings in her own home for the parents in her play-group so that they could plan what activities to offer the children and how to set them up. This extended to including neighbouring groups as they became established, and sharing what had been learned.

The desire to learn about how to enrich the lives of children and of their families was the foremost motivation that made PPA courses so popular over so many years. A secondary impetus came from the local authorities respon-sible for registering playgroups. These bodies, in many areas, set expectations for the training of the supervisors or play leaders. But the initial demand for courses came from a bottom-up direction, from parents who wanted to pro-vide the best they could for their children, both in playgroups and at home.

In the earliest days, the perspective was not one of training staff to be in charge of or run a playgroup. Learning needed to be a shared enterprise, with all the adults participating in the playgroup learning together how they could make their group work:

> The word we used was not 'training' but 'courses', which seemed more comfort-able and less threatening. (Meg Burford, tutor)

> The word 'training' was avoided like the plague. (Pat Kidd, fieldworker)

What mattered – as for the children in the groups – was the doing, not a paper product at the end of the learning process. The intended outcome of the courses (to use 21st century terminology) was the learning that had happened, not a qualification to undertake a specified role. What that learning might be would be different for each individual.

Some courses did begin to offer a record of attendance at the end, usually in response to the pressures from registering authorities to have some evidence that supervisors and leaders had attended a course with relevant content. But there was no attempt to assess what was being learned through homework, essays or course-work, and certainly not through exams.

The practice developed of tutors visiting course members' playgroups so they were able to observe if the opportunities to learn on the course were translated into changed practice in the group, but this did not constitute formal assessment of individuals' practice against standards. Sadly, tutors occasionally found that keen students were not able to transfer their new understanding and knowledge into practice in the group; sometimes the forces of 'we've always done it like this' were too strong to make room for change:

> Training courses without qualifications were the basis of our approach. (Joan Fazackerley, chair of PPA Training Committee)

The reasons for avoiding the concept of a qualification were expressed in various ways. The ethos of PPA courses was to start from where the course members were in their understanding and knowledge. The individuality of each person's previous experience and learning was acknowledged and valued. The aim was to move forward from that starting place at a pace and in ways that best suited a particular group of course members, not along a prescribed syllabus pathway. Each person's learning journey was seen as individual and they were encouraged to divert into learning byways led by their own interests. Attempting to assess that learning against predetermined objectives would therefore be unrealistic and not meaningful:

> A course sets out to support, enlighten and help ... Our job as tutors is not to try to force professional standards on mothers to 'bring them up to scratch'. We must help them to grow. (Brenda Crowe, national adviser 1970s)

> Everyone who tutors knows that learning is not a methodical, systematic, tidy, uniform or even accurately measurable process. The fallacy of assuming that one can pass people through a hierarchy of courses and that they will come out at the end of each stage equally capable or qualified must be recognised for the nonsense it is. (Margaret Brown, TDO 1978)

In addition, if assessment or examination were part of the course requirements, it could unbalance the focus of the course away from open and honest exchanges of experiences and opinions. It would also introduce the possibility of failing in topics so closely related to parenting as to risk suggesting that an unsuccessful course member might be a failure as a parent.

There was also a fear that a certificate of qualification might be seen as suggesting that someone was fully qualified and needed no further professional or personal development, complete anathema to PPA philosophy:

> There is a danger that a certificate can be seen as the seal on a piece of learning finished and done; as a result the 'qualified' student may conclude that she has learnt what there is to be learnt and therefore she need not go on learning and, as a qualified playgroup supervisor, she should stay in the job for many years to come. Such conclusions are clearly inimical to the student's personal growth, to the playgroup's growth and to the growth of the movement as a whole. (Mary Henderson, Scottish PPA, 1974)

PPA's moving on principle played an important part in this issue. If some individuals became qualified and assumed the leadership role in a group, there would be a block to the next generation of parents having the opportunity to run the sessions for their own children.

The 1974 Leicester Conference on Training, which brought together people from throughout PPA, unanimously rejected a qualification for play leaders, on the grounds that:

> a national qualification at play leader level is still held to be inappropriate. Such a qualification not only slows the turnover in leadership but could deny even the aspiration to leadership and responsibility.

There was resistance to the trend of increasing spurious professionalism and to the creation of a hierarchy of The Qualified and The Rest, undervaluing experience and personal attributes:

> We believe that the qualities of character, temperament, understanding, acceptance of parent and child, and the art of communication, all essential in a good play leader, do not lend themselves readily to objective testing methods. (Joan Fazackerley, chair of national Training Committee, 1974)

Many people mourn that this philosophy gradually faded. By the 1980s relationships within playgroups changed, with many parents accepting – indeed expecting – that staff would be employed to lead play sessions, even where committees of parents retained the management responsibility. This played a part in the seemingly inevitable shift towards qualifications.

Another factor at play in increasing the demand for qualifications came from those for whom PPA courses offered a chance truly to enjoy learning for the first time, following school careers which had left them with uncomfortable memories of being taught and also without the qualifications their abilities should have brought them. Having caught the learning bug through PPA courses and begun to build their self-confidence, they started to think that they would like something – a piece of paper – to prove to the world that they had abilities, which they now for the first time recognised in themselves. They challenged others in PPA who brought to their playgroup work their previous qualifications from life before parenthood, in spheres such as teaching:

> It's only you lot who have qualifications that think we who haven't don't need any. (Anonymous playgroup parent, 1980s)

This qualification-or-not debate also got caught up in the late 20th century drive in adult education towards qualifications for all, and defining learning largely in terms of that which could be measured and tested. The strength of those factors threatened PPA's focus on individual, personal learning.

Who? – the course members

In most areas, the earliest courses were attended not only by those who were taking on the role of leader of the playgroup and their assistants, but also by other parents, especially those who helped regularly in the group. Few play-groups were able to pay their leaders much – or indeed anything at all – so they frequently did not see themselves as staff, nor were they seen in that light by the other parents; everyone was on the equal footing of being a volunteer. If running the group was a co-operative endeavour, then joining a course was something to do together, a joint venture in pursuit of the knowledge and skills required to make playgroup a place where children and families flourished.

As we have seen, by the 1980s this early co-operative model was changing and leaders or supervisors were cast much more in the light of employed staff. As outside providers such as colleges became more involved, and courses tended to be more targeted at play leaders or supervisors, the importance of including parents from the playgroup so that everyone learned together was less under-stood. In addition, some local authorities were becoming more prescriptive about requiring leaders to attend specific training as part of the playgroup's registration:

> Avon County demanded 20 weeks be covered for the Playgroup Leaders' Course to be recognised by Social Services as a qualification for a playgroup leader. (Andrea Allez, fieldworker)

In the early days, everyone who joined a PPA course was there by choice – to learn about children and running playgroups. However, as attendance at a course became a requirement set by registering authorities, some course members – often from private playgroups with little parent involvement – attended under sufferance and their presence could unsettle a group if they were reluctant to participate actively:

> Two students were older than most of the others and myself and, at the first session, sat bolt upright and said they did not know why they had been sent because they'd been working with children for years. Not a very encouraging start. (Pat Kidd, tutor)

PPA courses were open to anyone interested in young children and in playgroups; there was no barrier in the form of previous training or qualifications being required. This meant that course groups included people with very different educational backgrounds who learned in different ways:

> ... from those who thankfully left school at the earliest possible moment to PhDs. Their (previous) jobs were anything from interesting and responsible careers and professions through to the dullest of dead-end jobs. (Joan Fazackerley, chair of PPA's national Training Committee 1974)

The common ground between them was their interest in and desire to learn about their children's development and how to provide stimulating play for them. For the most part, this produced a remarkable amount of cohesion within the group:

> The students were of mixed background and ability, but we didn't enquire about that – they were all parents of young children and their educational level didn't matter. (Helen Caldwell, tutor)

For many of those who came to PPA courses, this was the first time they had dipped their toe back into the ocean of learning since their school days. For some, memories of those days were not positive and they were consequently reluctant to repeat negative experiences of being on the receiving end of teachers and teaching and the sense of failure that exams had brought. The overwhelming majority of those who attended were women. Many had not succeeded at school, despite being capable, often because of the low expectations of their teachers or parents about what girls might achieve. Others whose formal education had been more positive had had the not uncommon experience of losing confidence following their transformation from capable and respected person in a work place to being 'just a mum'.

An element of courage was needed to embark on courses of any kind, especially if that meant going onto college premises, and some women had to contend with partners' reluctance for them to go out in the evenings on their own. But these opportunities were also exciting and challenging:

> For some people their school experience had been so negative that they were frightened of attending courses, and they needed lots of reassurance and often a friend to come too. (Sylvia Leathard, tutor)

> Even coming into Chorley in the evening on the bus was quite an ordeal; not many were drivers. Most people came in twos or threes. One very pretty young mum was only allowed to come by her jealous husband if two friends collected her and took her straight home afterwards. (Meg Burford, tutor)

> It was very exciting to go off in the car with another mum helper leaving my child asleep and husband in charge! I remember checking my tyres and head-lights to make sure the car would be OK! (Meg Bender, course member)

Besides summoning up the necessary impetus to join a course and navigate the logistics of getting there, sorting out family commitments, it has to be remembered that courses were not often entirely free, so would-be course members had also to find some money. Some playgroups fundraised to give their staff financial support towards course fees, but often the source was tight family budgets.

For many women who joined PPA courses, this was an open sesame to an unexpected world where learning was a pleasure. I always maintained that PPA courses should have carried a health warning: 'You may become addicted to learning'. Finishing a course left the question, 'What can I do next?' For some, this meant pursuing study and formal qualifications in related areas connected with children and families, such as teaching, psychology or social work. Others sought out learning in unrelated areas, but were always very clear that it was PPA courses that had inspired them to pursue new life and career pathways, having opened their eyes to the possibilities and opportunities to be grasped:

> Playgroup involvement is the first step to a lifelong learning situation for many. (Lady Plowden, PPA President 1970s)

A later chapter in this book recounts how PPA experiences influenced many women's lives after playgroups and PPA, through helping them to gain or regain confidence in themselves, new aspirations, skills of assertiveness, and a taste for self-development. Undoubtedly, PPA courses played a major role in this by opening up new horizons for learning and achieving and equipping participants to face – even seek – new challenges. In this way, PPA's important role in the women's movement was played out.

Who? – the tutors

As already described, early courses often emerged through informal exchanges of experience and ideas between the adults involved in neighbouring groups, often under the guidance or leadership of one of their number who had emerged as being knowledgeable about children and their development, perhaps because of their background in early years, based on their previous or current professional role. Some of these people did not perceive themselves as tutors:

> We preferred to call ourselves convenors, leaders or chairmen (not chairs in those days) rather than tutors. (Mary Heaps, tutor)

By the mid to late 1970s, a pattern was emerging of local PPA branches and county associations identifying experienced playgroup people with good communication skills, who had themselves attended some form of playgroup course, who could take on the role of tutor. These tutors were creative and flexible individuals who thoughtfully moulded courses to meet the learning needs of the course members who attended. They were motivated by the desire to introduce more parents to the playgroups' ideas about children's learning through play:

> Those of us who were involved in training were almost evangelical in our commitment to spread the PPA word. (Patsy Robinson, tutor)

This could have been a lonely and demanding role, so the practice of co-tutoring was widespread. Tutors supported one another, each playing to their strengths and developing their own area of expertise. Working in complementary roles, providing personal support to one another, they provided an example of part of the PPA ethos – reflecting, perhaps, the fact that it was an organisation composed mainly of women.

A model also emerged of an experienced tutor working in partnership with someone less experienced who could observe her co-tutor and be mentored or grown into a tutor – another PPA principle in action, enabling others to develop skills and experience and take on new roles.

Some courses were based on a model of bringing in several different experts in a variety of fields, organised by the tutor who linked their contributions. This produced a different dynamic in the relationship between tutor and course members, which needed to be secure and warm to enable the less outgoing course members to gain confidence and to participate. Many tutors began to observe that their students were less confident about making contributions to discussion when a different person appeared every week. In addition, not all such experts were good at communicating with playgroup people or presenting their specialist knowledge in ways relevant to playgroup situations. As tutors realised that they could use their own growing knowledge to cover the relevant topics and grew in confidence, the use of visiting speakers tended to diminish.

In some areas, local colleges of further education (FE), Adult Education (AE) centres and the Workers' Education Association (WEA) were involved from early on in the emergence of courses. Turning to a college for help was not without its problems. The innovative nature of playgroups meant that courses were effective when led by someone who had involvement in this emerging form of provision. But a college was more likely to want courses run under their aegis to be tutored by someone already on their staff. If these people were, for example, running the NNEB (Nursery Nurse Examination Board) courses, they might have relevant knowledge of young children, but many lacked any understanding either of playgroups or of teaching adults.

Some colleges parked playgroup courses in departments associated with what it was expected women would be interested in – cooking, flower arranging and dressmaking. Some proposals for who might be relevant teaching staff showed utter ignorance of the playgroup idea – such as the offer of the hairdressing lecturer who happened to have a spare period. A survey of playgroup courses carried out by Jonathan Brown of Newcastle University in 1973-4 showed that whilst 36 per cent of tutors had 'considerable playgroup experience', 24 per cent had 'little such experience'. Assumptions were sometimes made that because a person had a professional qualification related to working with young children, they would be a suitable tutor for playgroup courses. This was often not the case:

> One huge problem was that people thought you needed an expert to tutor the courses so all kinds of folk – headteachers, NNEB tutors, domestic science and nursing personnel, for example – with no direct knowledge of playgroups – some even of working with under-fives! – were employed. (Margaret Brown, TDO)

> A teaching or social work qualification alone is no guarantee that a tutor will be able to help playgroup people: practical knowledge of the actual problems that arise in a playgroup is essential. (Inner London PPA, 1976)

Strategies such as suggesting that an experienced playgroup person (not always paid) might tutor alongside the college member of staff gradually helped to shift some of these attitudes. Colleges became more ready to accept

PPA tutors and respect grew for the added value offered by tutors emerging from the playgroup movement.

The credibility of PPA tutors was derived from their being experienced and knowledgeable in playgroup practice. However, understandably, most colleges were not prepared to take onto their payroll someone not trained in teaching, however suitable they might be from a PPA point of view. The emergence of the longer and more complex Foundation Course in particular gave impetus to colleges' insistence that, if the course was to be funded from college resources, PPA tutors must have an adult education qualification. The 1974 Leicester Training Conference mentioned on page 49 recommended that the idea of a tutor qualification be taken forward.

This led to many aspiring tutors joining colleges' courses leading to the City and Guilds 730 Adult Education qualification. This often involved learning alongside would-be tutors in a wide range of vocational topics – car maintenance, yoga, furniture restoring, cake decorating, photography, upholstery and many more.

Taking on the role of tutor brought new learning experiences: the fascinating theories of how adults learn, learning styles, and practical ways of enhancing that learning. This learning derived not only from formal tutor-training, but also from sharing the learning experiences of the other students.

One responsibility often undertaken by county or regional training committees and PPA staff was to organise regular meetings of tutors. These offered opportunities for mutual support and for in-service training on emerging issues. Teachers' centres were often used as venues for these events, courtesy of supportive local authorities.

PPA tutoring was a jumping-off ground for some women's future employment. As colleges recognised the talent of PPA tutors to inspire learning and keep students engrossed, so offers of more employment in the college to teach a wider range of courses were forthcoming. And, if courses led to addiction to learning for many students, they also led to addiction to teaching for many tutors, as they experienced the immense satisfaction of seeing women flourish when new learning opportunities opened up their minds:

> I became passionate about the importance of giving adult learners, especially women, the confidence to believe in themselves. (Janet Bishop, tutor)

What? – the courses

The early courses might be more accurately characterised as workshops, often being arranged to address a specific need or interest amongst playgroup parents and leaders, without the expectation of a coherent series of sessions planned as a course.

During the 1960s, the idea of a linked series of sessions evolved and, by the early 1970s, introductory or basic courses were well established in many areas. These were of varying lengths – from six to twelve weekly sessions, each of two hours – with the overall aim of helping parents and play leaders to understand about children's development and how to provide play opportunities in playgroups. Thus they might include:

- ☐ the social, emotional, cognitive, communication and physical aspects of children's development; responding to children's behaviour

- ☐ the range of play provision such as sand and water, paint, clay and dough, junk and glue, imaginative play – including dressing up and role play – books, songs and rhymes, etc

- ☐ organisation of a playgroup – committee, finances, registration, safety.

As these courses whetted the appetite for more learning, and the demand for training play leaders and supervisors grew, the Foundation Course emerged during the 1970s. This was more broadly based, bringing in aspects such as parental involvement, and exploring in more depth how children develop and learn, as well as issues related to family structures, and provision for children in the local community. The intention was that the course should be the equivalent of one day a week for an academic year, but it was organised in different ways in different areas. For example, in the South West Region it was run in shorter sessions in a modular form of ten-week blocks.

As the Foundation Course became largely, though not exclusively, aimed at play leaders, so a different form of course for parents emerged: doorstep courses. These typically consisted of a short series of workshop-style sessions located, as the term 'doorstep' implies, in local playgroups – taking the courses to the parents, rather than expecting them to travel to the courses. These were generally practical sessions, and often included one about the value and need for the parent rota, and one about playing with the children without taking over their play. Thus there was a partial return to the original model of parents learning together. PPA's focus on learning opportunities for parents also continued with the collaboration with the Open University in the late 1970s in the development of *The Pre-school Child* Open University course.

Specialist courses and workshops also developed on, for example, music, committee work, mother and toddler groups and working with disabled children (children who had special needs). In some areas these specialisms were brought together in a further course.

In the 1980s, ILPPA began short courses on antiracism, starting a new agenda for playgroup courses, which spread slowly to other parts of the country and broadened into exploration of wider equality issues. It was typical of the PPA network's way of passing on good practice that in the mid-1980s, a tutor from London came to Wiltshire to run a workshop on antiracist concepts for local tutors and fieldworkers. The need to raise course members' awareness of equality issues across the range of gender, ethnicity, culture, disability, family and social background was given added impetus by the regulatory requirements of the Children Act 1989.

Fieldwork courses were designed for volunteers and staff, area organisers and branch visitors, who worked at local level. Their content included personal understanding and communication skills, relationships, working with groups or committees of experienced playgroup people who supported playgroups in a specific locality. In some areas, this was integrated with training tutors.

Courses were not the only learning opportunities on offer. Speakers at branch meetings and county conferences – which might also include workshops – could open up new ways at looking at a wide range of topics. PPA national staff and volunteers were generous in their readiness to travel to far-flung destinations at weekends to speak at conferences, often inspiring and reinvigorating playgroup people. And much learning happened in the playgroups themselves, as parents helped at sessions, and carried out various management and organisation roles on committees. See chapter 2 for more on this aspect of adult learning.

What? – the content
As we have seen, the origins of PPA courses lay in the desire of parents to learn how to run their playgroups to provide the best possible experiences for their children. The demand grew for opportunities to deepen this learning and also to learn about understanding families, discovering about other forms of early years provision and finding out about PPA itself.

As with so much else in PPA, no one sat down early in the organisation's history and worked out what the content of any of these courses should be; there was no centrally designed syllabus. The evolution of course content was organic: trial and error, listening and responding, flexibility and creativity all played a part in identifying what was helpful and appropriate to include.

For the most part, tutors had a high degree of autonomy in constructing early courses, although sponsoring agencies might want to exercise some supervision:

> I don't recall any syllabus being shown to us. We just worked out how we could best cover what we felt were the basic elements of running a group and tweaked it from term to term as experience showed us. (Viv Robson, tutor)

> I seem to remember having almost total freedom to plan these courses. There was a general oversight by Hampshire PPA and I believe each term's programme was at least shown to the sponsoring college. I think the LEA nursery or pre-school adviser may also have been aware of what we were doing, but I don't remember any direct intervention in the programme. (Mary Heaps, tutor)

> We had to submit a course programme to WEA for approval before we received any financial support. (Patsy Robinson, tutor)

An outline course programme might be drawn up by the tutor, but course members were invited to contribute suggestions and requests. Tutors often visited groups to find out what they needed and wanted to have included in courses. There was a balance to be achieved here between the merits of this sort of consultation and the tutor projecting knowledgeable confidence in what she could offer course members:

> One student objected to too much consultation about course content. 'How do I know what I don't know unless you tell me?' (Mary Heaps, tutor)

It could be demanding for tutors to be flexible enough to abandon a planned part of the course when it became apparent that course members' interests lay elsewhere:

> One tutor said to a course group after picking up a lack of interest in the topic, 'You don't want to know about this, do you? What do you really want to know about?' and she changed horses midstream, as it were. (Jean Ward, TDO)

This lack of a syllabus is partly explained by PPA's development in different ways at different rates in different places. But it was not just accidental; there was wariness about creating rigid, inflexible structures, which couldn't adapt to local needs and varying groups of course members:

> If we try to standardise the curriculum – ie work to a syllabus – there is always a danger that we will end up making sure we cover the syllabus rather than try to respond to the students' needs. (Margaret Brown, TDO 1978)

This lack of centralised uniformity was, of course, true to the spirit, especially the early spirit, of PPA, with its emphasis on responding to the needs of local playgroups and parents. However, the lack of direction also had a negative aspect, which became more apparent and more important to the reputation of PPA as time moved on. Some tutors tended to include in their courses only what they felt confident teaching, so some course members were denied the depth and breadth that the Guidelines indicated for the Foundation Course.

By the 1970s, in some areas regional and county training committees were beginning to construct course outlines – broad programmes of recommended content. But the emphasis remained on matching the course to the specific requirements articulated by the course members involved; a particular topic might be expanded or approached in a different way. The ideal remained to make courses fit the course members, not to attempt to fit the course members into a predetermined course:

> There was, as I recall, a common core of content for courses, with space built in for local issues and interests. (Susan Munns, tutor)

> No two courses were the same – overall structure and topics were the same but treatment was attuned to students' needs. (Elizabeth Belcher, tutor)

The 1974 Training Conference, whilst rejecting the idea of qualifications, gave the green light to the development of Course Guidelines for the Foundation Course. Many in PPA were involved in drawing up these Guidelines, so that existing good practice throughout the country could be drawn on. This was achieved amongst lively – sometimes heated, even passionate – debate. The significance of the resulting publication was that it represented an entirely new approach: guidance from the centre out to branches. It undoubtedly helped to establish a degree of consistency and thus parity across the country.

Guidelines for a Playgroup Foundation Course was published in 1975. In line with the avoidance of qualifications, an attendance certificate was recommended, not assessment, because, 'no course can guarantee a uniform level of knowledge or performance by its course members.' The necessity for tutors to be knowledgeable about playgroups, and to visit the course members' playgroups, was seen as a key factor in the quality of the course. The *Guidelines* recommended that the course be divided into three sections:

- ☐ The Family and the Child
- ☐ The Child and the Playgroup – the why and how of play activities
- ☐ The Playgroup and the Community.

The Guidelines look very light touch to 21st century eyes when we are used to so much direction from national level in every aspect of education. PPA principles were maintained by emphasising that these were guidelines, not a nationally set syllabus; local autonomy about how the course was delivered, and the detail of its content, was preserved. The introduction to the publication emphasised, 'There is no one right way, and no one person has all the answers':

> The following sections are written only to identify the various aspects that need to be considered, and integrated, on a Foundation Course, and are not intended to be taken word for word into session topics. (PPA *Guidelines for a Playgroup Foundation Course*, 1975)

Where and when?

The 1973-4 survey mentioned on page 54 referred to a range of places where the courses were held – FE colleges, schools, teachers' centres, university premises, clinics, private houses and even a playbus.

Where a PPA course was held was often a crucial factor in encouraging enrolment by potential course members. The venue needed to be somewhere where they would feel at ease. Apart from obvious access factors such as bus routes and the distances inevitable in rural areas, the message given by the choice of venue could be powerful. Colleges' involvement brought many advantages, but locating a course on college premises could be off-putting to those whose negative memories of education made them diffident about the idea of courses. Awareness also grew of the need to be aware of cultural sensitivities when using, for example, church premises.

Another factor was suitability for practical activities, as these might be messy and required space and furniture that could be moved and rearranged:

> The fact that the sixth-form college put us in an upstairs chemistry lab made it just that bit more convenient, especially for the sand and clay! (Ann Henderson, tutor)

The answer was often to use the premises occupied by a playgroup, so many PPA courses took place in village and church halls, and in community centres. The pros of this approach included being able to use the playgroup's equipment and materials, but cons often included the tiny chairs designed for the bottoms of small children, not those of adults!

The venues for fieldwork courses indicated the status those courses had earned. They were frequently held in teachers' centres, or even on university outreach premises.

The timing of courses was a topic for lengthy debate. Holding the course during the day meant starting after and finishing before school delivery and pick-up times, but that could still enable lengthy sessions. But what about mothers with young, pre-school children? One or two small children, especially babies, might be accommodated in course sessions but several would present problems. Premises would not always enable a crèche to be held alongside the course room, and in any case many course members were not comfortable about the idea.

One region suggested that mothers should find a family member or friend to care for their child while they attended a course and, if that was not possible, postpone the course until their youngest child was older. (Some might characterise that attitude as paternalism or, perhaps more appropriately, 'maternalism'.) In contrast, in 1986 PPA Southern Region produced a booklet *On Course Together* that offered advice and ideas for provision for children alongside courses and meetings. This could enable the participation of a wider group of parents, so long as careful attention was also paid to the quality of the children's experiences.

Evening courses could solve the childcare problem in two-parent families, but single parents, or those with partners whose work meant they were often absent or who worked irregular hours, might prefer daytime sessions. Evening sessions were usually restricted to two to two and a half hours, whilst daytime sessions could run for three to four hours. Constant reconsideration of timing, and consulting potential course members, produced adjustments and refinements – but there was never a fits-all solution. The 1973-4 survey revealed that 32 per cent of courses were held during the day.

How? – funding and organisation

Courses required resources – venues, tutors' time, equipment and materials. Some of this might be provided from various sources in kind, but it became apparent that, to sustain courses for the future, it would be necessary to put them on a properly funded footing. At various times in various places, course members themselves paid towards these costs, but efforts were always made to keep fees as low as possible; most of those enrolling on courses were not employed people so had little or no income of their own, and any contributions they made came out of their family budgets.

An example of in kind resourcing was the venues that were made available by statutory bodies. The earliest courses were often held on the premises of one of the playgroups involved, but local authorities and other agencies began to offer venues free of charge, such as rooms on health premises or in schools. The costs of the use of the venue were absorbed by the relevant agency, rather than their making a grant to PPA. The death knell for using school premises without charge came in the late 1980s with the move towards local management of schools, with each handling its own budget; while the local education authority might be prepared to underwrite the costs of heating and caretaker time, individual schools could not justify spending money in ways not directly for the benefit of the children on their roll, however sympathetic head-teachers and governors might be towards pre-school provision.

Tutors of early courses were rarely paid, but as support was forthcoming in the 1970s from FE colleges, AE centres and the WEA, tutors who had adult education qualifications began to earn hourly rates in line with other part-time FE teachers, which – in theory at least – were set at a rate that took into account preparation time. Co-tutoring sometimes meant a fee for only one tutor, so it had to be split between the two. What might look on paper like reasonable rates of pay for tutors were often eroded in various ways.

Visiting professionals such as speech and language therapists, librarians or child psychologists might come along and contribute to a course as part of their job, but inviting, for example, the leader of the local opportunity group to talk about working with disabled children might mean that the tutor gave up her fee for that session in order to pay the speaker. This became more of an issue by the end of the 1980s when local authority and health agencies began to monitor budgets more closely and began to expect their staff to be paid a fee for contributing to PPA courses, sometimes at rates far beyond the capacity of course budgets.

Equipment such as projectors (later, video players) was often borrowed from WEA local offices, teachers' centres or schools, some of which also duplicated (later, photocopied) handouts. Branches often fundraised to buy or hire slides or films (later, videos), such as the ten-minute silent films produced by PPA which showed children engaged in play with dough and clay, dry and wet sand, and paint.

When courses were held away from college premises, access to libraries could be a problem, especially in rural areas. To overcome this, some county library services provided the free loan of book boxes filled with background reading relevant to a particular course; course members signed out a book they wanted to read and returned it at a later session.

Playgroups or the branch toy library might be the source of children's books and play equipment on loan to be used to provide examples for some course sessions. Materials such as clay or paint for practical sessions might also be provided by playgroups, or through branch bulk-buy schemes, and scrap stores could offer junk, but many tutors raided their own kitchen cupboards for the flour, salt and oil to make dough. One of my own recollections of being a tutor is that setting out for course sessions often involved loading the boot of the car with the book box, ingredients for dough or junk play or painting, plus coffee, tea, milk and sugar, and even the kettle from my kitchen.

PPA courses became popular with many FE colleges, valued for their good enrolment rates and high retention rates, which were critical for colleges' funding; students attended most sessions right to the end of the course, in contrast to the high drop-out rates which characterised many FE courses. PPA also endeared itself to colleges by publicising the course and finding the students and, when courses were held away from college premises, carrying out the course administration, such as enrolment. What also became apparent to colleges was that their enrolment figures for other courses also grew when playgroup courses whetted appetites for personal development and continued learning, especially when playgroup courses were held on college premises. By 1975, over 450 colleges offered playgroup courses.

Some local authorities – often the education department – became willing to contribute to the funding of some courses. An example of a pattern of funding might be:

☐ doorstep or basic and introductory courses funded by the local authority or WEA, or from PPA branch fundraising activities

☐ the Foundation Course resourced by FE colleges or AE centres, providing the premises and paying the tutors

☐ specialist workshops or courses such as working with disabled children funded by the local authority – possibly the social services department.

Putting together these sorts of patchworks of funding and support in kind took persistence and clear communication skills on the part of PPA volunteers and staff, sometimes with support from the individuals in the local authority responsible for registering playgroups. TDOs played a leading role in these negotiations alongside county level PPA staff and volunteers. Often a break-through occurred when a sympathetic individual in a local authority or college got the message about the role of playgroup courses in the adult education world and became a champion for supporting these courses:

> The Head of FE described the playgroup movement as being 'as much about the education of mothers as individuals as about the education of children.' After that we always had great support from adult education. (Mary Heaps, local training committee member)

As the volume and type of different courses increased, careful and continuous planning became needed to identify which courses to run in which locations at which times. Foundation Courses were usually planned by a training committee at county level in negotiation with colleges, and supported by PPA at regional and local level, but branches often planned and organised doorstep or basic courses. In 1974, Scottish PPA published *Organising a playgroup course for the first time*, emphasising that setting up a course could not be done in a hurry – the careful planning and co-ordination with other agencies essential to get everything required in place took time.

How? – methods

The style of teaching on PPA courses was always high on practical content and on opportunities for course members to exchange information, ideas and opinions through discussion.

Tutors did not just tell course members what activities should be provided in a playgroup; they encouraged them to experience the activities for themselves – pummelling dough or clay, making models and collages with junk and glue, painting, pouring water and sand. Thus they could gain insight into the value of children's play that was not subject to direction, but developed or lingered where the child wanted it to go or stay:

> I remember one student saying how she now appreciated what it was like for the children when they were told to stop doing an activity in which they were engrossed – she felt quite miffed at being told to clear away the practical activity she was enjoying. (Helen Caldwell, tutor)

> Mothers enjoyed role-playing a story circle and experiencing the different methods of telling stories. On one occasion, after listening with total absorption, a mother said eagerly as the story ended, 'Read it again!' (Jean Ward, TDO)

Such practical, hands-on explorations made it easier for the quieter, less confident members of the course group to speak to a fellow course member when they were alongside one another, each engaged in their own play.

Tutors sought to draw out the knowledge and understanding already present in the course group. It was a given that each course member could make a contribution, providing new perspectives for others. Readiness to share experiences and even feelings in an open way requires a culture of trust; to make the development of such trust possible, tutors sought to foster a warm, relaxed, informal atmosphere in course sessions:

> There was an overall thread, running through both the content of the course and the approach to teaching, of respect for all: no one was a failure; everyone – adults and children – could grow and develop at their own rate and could contribute. (Meg Bender, tutor)

Small group discussion was a frequently used technique, with careful attention being paid to mixing the membership of each group so that over-enthusiastic or dominant individuals did not drown out the more tentative comments and suggestions of the less assertive. People who were already friends were usually distributed into different discussion groups to lessen the appearance of cliques.

Triggers for discussion might be problems or scenarios to be considered and explored from a range of perspectives. This enabled course members to explore their own understanding and ideas, based on their own experience and previous learning, as well as hearing alternative approaches from others. This respect for what each person brought to the course was a key element in developing course members' self-esteem. Their experience of being 'just a mum' might not have attracted much respect in other contexts in society, but on a playgroup course, it was acknowledged and valued.

Formal settings were not conducive to such practical and discussion methods, so preparing a room for a course session often meant furniture removal was a required aspect of the tutor's role:

> The basement of the old grammar school where the College was based was initially set out with tables and chairs in a very formal way. We soon changed that to a friendly circle. (Meg Burford, tutor)

Coffee breaks were seen as an essential ingredient in the mix of a course session, giving opportunities for one-to-one chat and the flowering of friendships.

Anyone walking in to a room where a PPA course was in full flow could not miss the buzz, the sense of enjoyment, of having fun. More careful observation would reveal the intensity of some of the exchanges and experiences. This mix of enjoyment and depth was perhaps what captivated so many people, the source of their growing addiction to learning:

It was intensely 'real' learning and therefore enduring. (Margaret Perry, course member)

The legacy

Training for people involved in playgroups continued to evolve and change, much affected by changes in further and adult education and the effects that changes in family life and the wider society had on early years provision. The tighter regulation introduced by the 1989 Children Act also played a part. The guidance to the Act required that 'at least half the staff should hold a recognised qualification in daycare or education, or have completed a training course specified by the Pre-school Playgroups Association (PPA) or other voluntary body'. It was a coup for PPA to have its courses recognised in this way, and the Diploma in Playgroup Practice, which was awarded on the basis of formal assessment, emerged in 1991 to meet the requirement.

We could debate whether those changes were for better or worse, but we can profitably reflect from our 21st century perspective on what has been lost, and what we might seek to regain, that was captured by the PPA philosophy of adult learning:

- ☐ start the learning journey where people are now
- ☐ value and build on what their previous experience of life has revealed to them and the contribution each can make
- ☐ move forward along paths that are indicated by individuals' interests; avoid confining learning to a rigidly dictated programme
- ☐ don't let attempts to assess and measure learning divert attention from nurturing learning and personal development.

This underpinning philosophy of learning provided the fertile context for extending the original playgroup model into a variety of social settings and meeting the needs and requirements of a range of families.

And it can be contended that this should also be the philosophy we should embrace more wholeheartedly for young children's learning.

Note

Unless otherwise specified, the quotations in this chapter are taken from communications elicited from several people during 2010; the roles given are those held at the time to which the quotation refers.

4

Playgroups in the community
Meg Burford

with contributions from Ann Henderson,
Linnet McMahon and Charlotte Williamson

The energetic and innovative approach that characterised the early days of the playgroup movement did not stop with playgroups. People who had gained confidence from knowing that they had made a difference, and who had acquired useful skills and experience, both from courses and from their ongoing battle to get playgroups established, naturally continued to address needs and issues as they found them, often on a strictly local basis.

PPA people were free to develop new initiatives because the bottom-up nature of the organisation did not impose any constraints from above. Membership provided a supportive framework, and colleagues to work with, without any limiting injunctions or imposed structures from on high. A group of local people could identify a need, decide to do something about it and – often in a remarkably short time – act on their decision. Some initiatives naturally took longer than others, but lessons that had been learnt from their struggles to start playgroups stood members in good stead when they turned their attention to the needs of children and families in other areas. They approached community situations with the expectation that if something needed doing, they might well be able to do it. The impact of the developing playgroup movement reached into many organisations and communities in ways that could never have been foreseen. Chapters 1 and 2 described how playgroups were set up and how they worked. This chapter aims to chart some of the many spin-offs into the wider community.

Parent and toddler groups

One of the most exciting spin-offs was the growth of mother and toddler groups. These started to emerge in the late 60s when mothers with under-threes said, 'Why can't we come too?' In addition, parents discovering beneficial new approaches to child rearing once their children started playgroup often wished most fervently that they could have accessed the same information and experiences when their child was much younger. The established playgroup did not fit the needs of babies and toddlers because it was designed primarily for three-to-five year olds, most of whom were ready to be left, at least for a while, without their parents or main carers. So the parents of the under-threes, like the Little Red Hen, said, 'We'll do it ourselves', and they did.

These informal organisations had many names, including parent and toddler groups, mother and baby groups, and pram clubs, and their rapid growth suggests how great the need for them had been. There were an estimated 4,000 by 1977. They lobbied PPA for recognition and support, which came in the form of a national working group set up in 1975; this led in 1977 to the formally established PPA Working Party on Mother and Toddler groups, a project funded by Barclays Bank in 1975. It included members from all the regions in England and Wales as well as a link from the Health Visitors' Association and representation from the Baptist Church, the Catholic Church, the Church of England's Board of Social Responsibility, the Methodist Church through its Young Wives' Groups, the Salvation Army, the Society of Friends and the United Reformed Church. After an extensive survey of 1,702 groups the report, published in 1978, found:

> The isolation of the young mother ... has lasting effects on individuals and their families and thereby on society at large ... Society can reap rich rewards from co-operative support, which helps towards happy, relaxed families. (PPA Report on Mother and Toddler Groups, 1978)

The report also called on PPA 'to undertake support work ... to cover the additional demands of the mother and toddler movement.' At the 1981 AGM in Newcastle, the resolution 'that PPA gives equal consideration to mother and toddler groups and playgroups' was passed by a huge majority. From then on parent and toddler groups became increasingly if slowly embedded in the PPA world. PPA's leaflet *Welcome to the Mother and Toddler Group* defined what they were and what they did:

> All these groups are about meeting people, making friends, sharing ideas and anxieties too! Those who go are mums and dads with their babies, toddlers and

pre-schoolers. Groups also welcome mums-to-be, others who care for small children and anyone who would like to help.

Mother and Toddler Groups offer a place to meet ... most groups run once or twice a week in a hall, clinic, community centre, school or home. They provide a warm, safe, relaxed setting where parents can enjoy a cup of tea and a chat while the children play nearby. The parents remain responsible for their children at all times. A small charge is usually made to cover the cost of rent, insurance, heating and drinks.

The groups were very popular:

It was a high spot in the week ... nothing seemed as awful as it had done when I went out.

It saved me from bashing her. (PPA *Report on Mother and Toddler Groups*, 1978:14)

In the rest of this chapter the term 'PPA groups' is used as shorthand to include both playgroups and parent and toddler groups. It also includes under-fives groups which were often the answer in villages when there were insufficient children to separate out the ages. Parents or carers stayed with the under 3s while the 3-5s enjoyed the playgroup facilities with the play leaders. As more women started going back to work, some children would come with their carer – childminder, nanny or granny – who also benefited from the company of the other adults in the group.

In this village, the whole family is usually involved, and much of the equipment is made by dads and granddads. (PPA *Report on parent involvement in playgroups*, 1980:15)

Inclusion in community playgroups

Early playgroups were about mothers in the same neighbourhood, village or local area getting together to organise a playgroup close to home, usually within walking distance. Travelling further afield was not a realistic possibility, unless you were on a bus route, for few mothers had use of a car. The whole family had access to the playgroup; brothers and sisters went together (younger ones perhaps to the mother and toddler group). The playgroup became an important part of the neighbourhood and community in which each family found its place, and often its means of support – as the African proverb says, 'It takes a whole village to rear a child.' So it was a logical next step for a family with a child who had a physical disability such as cerebral palsy or blindness or a more all-embracing condition such as Downs or autism to look for the playgroup's support. These days, thankfully, such a family's expectation would be taken for granted. Difference is better understood and accepted as part of the human condition. But then playgroups that responded were pioneering, both in including families with children who had special needs and in meeting their needs for play.

The old attitude to learning disability (mental handicap) was that the children were ineducable and so were best put away, out of sight and out of mind, many in long-stay hospitals (painfully described in Maureen Oswin's *The Empty Hours*, whose revelations contributed to their eventual closure). Children with physical disabilities were little better treated, sent off to special boarding schools. 'Luckier' ones were bussed off to training centres and special schools. By the 1960s there was more understanding of the damage to young children of long separation from their mothers. The Robertsons' films demonstrating the distress of children alone in hospital gave strength to the campaign for parents' rights first to visit and later to stay with their children. In parallel, growing numbers of more confident and informed parents insisted both on keeping their 'special' child at home and also on that child's right to education. The local playgroup was the natural place to start, where parents hoped to find acceptance, companionship and some practical help.

Adults in the playgroup needed to confront their own fears about how to talk to the parents and how to provide safe and stimulating play. In rising to the occasion, they not only gave the family desperately needed support but also learned, as did the playgroup children, to see the child first and the disability second – as something to be managed not pitied. 'The special needs are extra ones, not alternative ones, to those all children share' (PPA *Guidelines for Playgroups with a Handicapped Child*, 1975):

> I have a vivid memory of staff and helpers in a church hall group ingeniously padding all the corners of their trestle tables in preparation for accepting a child with haemophilia. The parents had consulted their medical advisers, had helped in what would now be called a risk assessment, and were determined that their son would attend normal educational facilities. I remember also the celebrations in the same group when a little Downs girl achieved sufficient bladder control in the daytime to attend the group in ordinary knickers. She was still flashing her knickers at me in supermarkets several years later! (PPA area organiser, 1980)

Parents with previous specialist experience could support the playgroup in making parents feel welcome and included rather than rushing to offer respite, even if this would be helpful at some later point. 'It may meet the mother's needs better for her to feel free to stay and chat, or just watch, than be over-encouraged to have a break' (Dr Jane Grubb, 1970). What's more, in-clusion needed to contain some element of a feeling of a parent being res-ponsible for their child and the group, whether or not they stayed, or joined in and helped, or went on a committee. Parents who found that they could give as well as receive grew in self-respect and confidence. They, like their children,

> ... have to grow up and live in a normal community, and the sooner they become integrated into that community the easier it is for them and their families. The aim should be to get the children to think of themselves as part of the community, doing what all the other children do, not to regard themselves as something special and odd. (*Guidelines for Playgroups with a Handicapped Child* 1975)

One group found a granny to come in as an extra person when a little girl who had Downs Syndrome joined them, but the child herself was just part of the group, as was her mother.

Children achieved very satisfying levels of autonomy and self-esteem through their acceptance in an ordinary playgroup. Other children and their parents learned not to be frightened of difference but to appreciate a child for who he or she was. By the end of the 1970s about one in four playgroups had at least one child with a disability.

Play and autonomy
Self-directed play is essential to the development of a child's autonomy (see Chapter 2) and to their sense of self, and self-esteem. Children with physical and learning disabilities have less autonomy in their lives and so have greater need for self-directed play. Yet all too often they receive structured learning programmes, which risk taking away their autonomy still further. The play-group's opportunities and stimulus for spontaneous play with natural materials, alongside or with other children, were precious. For the playgroup adults it was a challenge to find ways for a child to reach and choose what to play with, but the standard playgroup fare of dough, paint, sand and water play (occasionally safer substitutes such a bowl of pasta, or conkers and autumn leaves) provided the sensory responsive materials that encourage playing. Home-corner play (and a soft doll or teddy) fostered pretend and symbolic communication, especially with an adult around to respond to the tiniest cues from the child without taking over. Treasure baskets (containing small everyday objects to look at, feel, smell and listen to) would absorb an immobile child. We learned from parents too:

> An unemployed father came into the playgroup with his cerebral palsied son. Everyone watched in astonishment as the child who had been gently lifted from place to place roared with delight in a rough and tumble romp on the floor with his dad. (*Contact,* March 1973)

Above all, the companionship, familiarity and friendships with other local children were of lasting value.

Mutual benefits

We think of children with special needs gaining from entry to ordinary groups, and of course they do, but the benefits are mutual. Other members of the group learn things about the variety of the human condition and about practical ways to adapt to one another:

> In one group, on the days when a very popular little boy severely limited by spina bifida attended, the children – with no prompting at all from the adults – transferred the focus of their play to floor level. They were not being kind; they simply wanted the play to work. (PPA tutor, private communication, 1974)

There is also the question – for the adults, at least – of the fresh perspective that can be introduced through the presence of somebody whose life is not going to go the way of other children's lives:

> In a group I used to visit, a terminally ill child celebrated with glee a fourth birthday nobody had thought he would reach. (He died shortly afterwards.) His parents had gone to endless trouble to keep him in the group for almost all of his short life and there were clear implications for people thinking about the objects of pre-school education – or, by extension, all education. His parents did not bring him because they wanted him to 'get on'. They didn't want him to get where he was going at all. They brought him because they wanted his life to be as rich and full as they could make it for as long as it lasted. It seems very sad that a child has to be dying before such a clear and simple criterion can apply, and the parents in the group were aware of this; I heard them talking about it occasionally. (PPA branch chair, private communication, 1981)

Opportunity playgroups

One disadvantage of community playgroups was that children needed to be nearing three years old to attend. Families with a child with a disability or long-term illness needed support much earlier than that. Parents, in particular, needed advice and friendship from the time their child was diagnosed, often at birth. While parent-toddler groups might be available, and some gave good support, it could be painful for parents to join in the chat about milestones children had reached when their own child might be on a slower or very different developmental path. Many such parents, who could feel very vulnerable and isolated, first needed a place where they could meet other parents in the same boat, be open about their feelings and give one another mutual support.

Parents wanted their children – their child with difficulties and also brothers and sisters, who had their own emotional needs – to have creative and stimulating play opportunities in an environment where each child was valued and understood. An opportunity group, with its mixture of children with and without disabilities, could meet these needs. Groups provided the usual playgroup activities: play with natural materials, cutting and sticking, pretend play, books and stories, sometimes physical play in soft play areas. Singing action songs together, parents joining in, gave a sense of belonging to a community.

Parents also appreciated information and advice from empathetic and practical professionals, preferably in a one-stop shop rather than the endless round of appointments to see different people. Professional workers learned from observing children and meeting parents in a more relaxed and familial setting. It made for a more equal parental partnership with professionals, who 'get this training but they don't really know how you feel'. There was some specialist provision, such as groups run by Mencap or other organisations offering help with specific disabilities, but the decision to attend required parents' acknowledgment of their child's condition, which could be a slow, painful process more easily supported in an opportunity group. As parents regained confidence, often after becoming involved in helping in the group, or in organising it, they might choose in due course to move back to their local playgroup or nursery:

> This is a great relief to them. In some ways, helping each other heals a wound that has been caused by always being on the receiving end of help. (Pat Hughes, *Oxtale*, 1979).

Opportunity groups – originally known as opportunity classes – started when Dr Ron Faulkner, a GP in Stevenage, was approached by the mother of three-year-old twins, one of whom had Down's syndrome. The mother wanted to provide playgroup opportunities for both her children without separating them, so in 1966 the Stevenage opportunity class opened, welcoming families with children with developmental problems and disabilities. Brothers and sisters without disabilities came too.

The spontaneous local growth of such groups (by 1980 there were more than 150), accompanied by informal contact by correspondence and a wish for some centralisation and guidance, led to unanimous agreement at an early conference of the opportunity group movement that its future development should take place within the auspices of PPA. Dr Faulkner, reporting to PPA's *Opportunities Grasped* conference in 1978, thanked the playgroup movement, on behalf of the early opportunity group campaigners, for their 'welcome, tolerance, advice and practical help'.

PPA's Subcommittee on Handicap was later incorporated into the Special Needs Committee, which in 1974 acquired a specialist national adviser, ensuring that provision for children with illness and disabilities continued to be seen as a community-based activity within the mainstream of provision for all children. PPA produced helpful publications – *Guidelines for a Playgroup with a Handicapped Child, The Handicapped Child and his Mother in the Playgroup, Notes for Opportunity Groups*, and *Focus* sheets on specific needs – while PPA courses could help with the thinking about how best to include families. PPA provided the facilitating environment (see chapter 2) for the playgroups, which then provided this for the parents, enabling them in turn to offer greater emotional holding for their children, both those with a disability and their brothers and sisters. The wider benefit, however, was to the whole community's understanding and acceptance of difference.

Play in hospital

PPA members' belief in play led them to offer themselves, their advice and their funds to hospitals soon after the first play schemes in children's wards were started by Save the Children Fund in 1963. By 1972, 50 out of 200 PPA branches had taken some initiative to provide or promote play in any local hospitals that had children's wards (unpublished PPA survey, October 1972). They started play schemes in acute wards, in long-stay and mental handicap (learning disability) hospitals, and for the children of outpatients or of parents visiting their sick child or other relative. Children of all ages were included. Schemes had voluntary or salaried play leaders or both. Large numbers of playgroup supervisors and rota mothers volunteered: 30 at Sutton Coldfield, 48 at Scarborough, 50 at York. The days of the week and the hours worked varied from hospital to hospital. Play material and salaried play leaders were funded by the PPA branch or by the hospital or by both. The National Association for the Welfare of Children in Hospital (NAWCH) ran similar play schemes, some jointly with PPA branches.

Difficulties abounded in the early days. Some hospitals refused all offers of help. Others imposed restrictions: 'The one hour the hospital allows us to come...'. 'Routine must not be affected and children are not allowed toys in bed after we have gone.' PPA members believed that salaried play leaders giving continuity of relationships to the children, their parents and the nursing staff were better in the stressful environments of children's wards than rotas of voluntary play leaders. (They also wanted to practise what they preached about mothers being with their own children outside playgroup or school hours.) But rotas of voluntary play leaders were excellent when continuity did not matter. Even salaried play schemes could fall short of full-day cover, though, because of difficulties fitting in with consultants' rounds. Further difficulties arose when branches had to ask the hospital to take over the funding of the play leader and the play materials, and a few play schemes had to come to an end. On the other hand, some hospitals became so convinced of the value of play that they funded play schemes willingly when branches' money ran out.

As well as setting up PPA play schemes, PPA members worked as volunteers in NAWCH play schemes and in schemes organised by the hospitals themselves. Out in the community, some playgroups liaised with their local hospital, taking child outpatients (Poole) or long-stay inpatients (Stoke Mandeville) into the playgroup as part of their treatment. Some nurses and play leaders attended PPA branch courses (Bristol, Hull) or seminars (York). With NAWCH, some PPA branches put on conferences on play in hospital to which they invited paediatricians and ward sisters.

PPA branches and individual members made these commitments primarily from their belief in the value of play. But they were also deeply concerned about many of the policies and practices in hospitals and they saw the gifts they made of their time, their work and the funds they raised as a constructive path to reform. Many hospitals in the 1960s, 70s and 80s restricted visiting by parents, in spite of guidance from the Department of Health and Social Security that said that parents should have access to their children throughout the 24 hours of every day. Thus the stated aim of one play scheme, a voluntarily-funded, purpose-built playroom in the hospital grounds, was to provide a supervised, safe, enjoyable place where children could enrich their experience through play while their parents visited their sick brother or sister in the children's ward.

The scheme's unstated but not secret aims were to demonstrate the value of play to ward staff; to show them that they could use dough, damp sand and other play material on the ward; to persuade ward staff to allow children from the playroom to visit their siblings on the ward; to gain children's entry into adult wards to see their parent, uncle, aunt or grandparent ('Ask if you can show granny your painting'); and above all, to secure unrestricted visiting for parents. These aims were, in time, achieved (Williamson, 2010). Many PPA play schemes found that example and good relationships with senior staff could do a lot to change attitudes and practices, even in unpromising institutions.

Creating a national voice is always important (Henderson, 1978). In 1971 PPA, NAWCH and Save the Children Fund set up a national liaison committee to co-ordinate work on play in hospitals, to discuss training for play leaders and to disseminate information (Hogg, 1990). Play specialists funded by the NHS are now routine in children's wards; but the links to the community and the opportunities for friendly surveillance of hospitals' policies and practices and, if necessary, their constructive subversion, have been lost.

Traveller families

In parts of the country visited by Travellers, their children came to the attention of local playgroup people. These children and their families faced many challenges in their lives. Due to their itinerant lifestyle there was no access to the normal services for under-fives. Health care was sporadic and when accessed there would be no continuity of care. There was cultural marginalisation of Travellers' families, which was due partly to the resident population's fear of the unknown and lack of knowledge of the Traveller culture. In many communities the arrival of Travellers was seen as a threat because of competition for employment and suspected petty thieving. Facilities for Travellers in and around towns were often very poor and the police would impose frequent and unexpected moves on the families and insist that they relocate from one local authority patch to another.

Owing to the closeness of Travellers' family units, their children would have very little experience of adults outside the family and of being in accommodation other than caravans.

The first approach to PPA often came from Travellers who regularly visited the same part of the country for seasonal work and became concerned about their children's access to the education system. It was slow work to gain the confidence of the children and adults. The children had never been away from their mothers before and the adults tended to be wary of anything that smacked of authority. Where playgroup experience was provided on the

Travellers' site it took great ingenuity to adapt playgroup provision to suit the circumstances:

> I set up play materials outside or occasionally inside a caravan used for sleeping. On one occasion we set up inside a derelict house with parents working to clear the floor space. Sadly the Travellers were moved on by the local authority and police before we could make more progress. (Regional Fieldworker's Report, 1979)

In some areas Traveller parents showed an interest in learning more about play and in developing their own literacy skills to be able to support their children's education. They were also keen to take driving tests.

PPA people involved in this work learned to adapt play opportunities to acknowledge the children's previous experiences, and in some areas showed great resourcefulness as they worked to ensure that the pictures, books, dressing-up clothes and home-play equipment in the playgroup reflected the lives and homes of the Traveller children as well as those of the resident population.

In areas where a playbus was available, offering peripatetic playgroup provision, it was often used to great advantage. PPA used the buses to take play opportunities directly to the children. Some children and families, having gained confidence through their welcome on the bus, then went on to use pre-school facilities off the Travellers' site.

Refugee families

PPA people responded also to the plight of refugees arriving in this country. These were often young families who, uprooted from everything they knew and after a terrifying journey, found themselves in a strange place where absolutely nothing was familiar: food, clothes, language, customs or weather. Parents struggling with these changes were also simultaneously having to try to support traumatised children.

In 1972 it was PPA people who equipped and staffed play facilities in transit camps used by Asian families expelled from Uganda. The much-needed opportunities for the children to play also gave the parents an opportunity to have some time on their own to begin to cope with the challenges of settling in a strange country.

Later, a similar service was organised for the children of the fleeing Vietnamese boat people. Many of these children could not at first bear to be parted from their mothers and, in a safe situation for the first time, some of the children used the playgroup equipment in distressing ways, to act out the ugly experiences that had brought them to this country.

Later still, PPA members were involved with refugee families from Kosovo. Initially these groups comprised all children, from toddlers to young teenagers, but schooling was later provided for the over-fives so the groups became more manageable in size. Volunteers worked hard to improve the children's English and to help them adapt to local customs and expectations so that their stay in the UK was a better experience. The facilities provided fun, learning and some structure for the children in what could have been endless days.

When the families left temporary accommodation they were often assimilated into local playgroups with the help of the PPA network. This invaluable humanitarian work could be very demanding for the people involved but was also very rewarding.

Children in prisons

Prisons may seem an unlikely setting for PPA influence but once again PPA people's concern for young families and their children led to action – initially in Hull and Brixton.

Women wanting to visit their husbands or partners in prison frequently came long distances using public transport with several young children. A PPA branch chairman who was a taxi driver experienced at first hand the distress of young mothers arriving in a strange town with tired, hungry and stroppy children who did not understand what was going on. They all found themselves in an unfamiliar and unwelcoming environment. The mothers were anxious to see their partners and share their concerns and problems with them as well as hearing how the partners were faring. They also wanted their children to behave well so that they would not attract the attention of the prison officers or distract other families or let their partners down. The children might not recognise their fathers or want anything to do with them and were fidgety and bored. PPA decided that things could be improved and mooted the idea of play facilities at the prison.

Initially many prison officers were against the idea. Prisons were not meant to be brightly coloured happy places, they said, and indulging criminal families was not part of their brief. Once they had seen the alleviation of the children's distress and the improvement of the quality of the visits, opinions changed.

As well as organising play opportunities for visiting children in many prisons, PPA people were involved in women's prisons where there were mother and baby units. In one area, an initial approach was made to provide one session for women prisoners in a playgroup:

> At the end of the session it was hard to realise that these women were not going back to their own children but to prison. (Alison Jones, writing in *Contact*, February 1985)

This led to regular sessions on courses for women in the prison, which were very practical and popular:

> We made dough and talked. Dough always brings memories and helps people talk. Most of the women seemed to have had such sad lives and fallen through every net. (PPA tutor, personal letter)

Another development came from an invitation to visit a prison mother and baby unit. The result was a regular four-times-weekly mother and toddler group in the prison itself. These sessions, although demanding for the leader, were very successful, and led to a branch-approved doorstep course (see chapter 3), which enabled women who had never achieved anything at school to show that they had achieved something in prison.

Women's refuges

The plight of children who found themselves suddenly uprooted due to domestic violence and living in unfamiliar surroundings with their trauma-tised mothers had some features in common with the situation of children in prisons. PPA members sought both to ease distress and to minimise its impact by providing play opportunities in many women's refuges. As in the prisons, what PPA members offered was non-judgemental, practical support combined with absolute discretion.

These initiatives were summed up by a PPA tutor:

> In the best playgroup tradition we hope to be able to spot a need, identify it and do something about it. (*Contact*, February 1985)

Armed forces families

One of PPA's most extensive outreach activities was in the armed forces playgroup world. The armed forces developed playgroups with customary efficiency and by 1977 there was extensive playgroup provision in many esta-blishments embracing all three services – the Army, the Navy and the Royal Air Force. The provision was efficient, but the forces are accustomed to pro-viding for their families and had failed to grasp the concept of parental involvement.

The common pattern for forces' playgroup provision both in the UK and abroad was that children were bussed into playgroups by service transport.

No mothers were allowed on the vehicles for insurance reasons and the playgroups often met at some distance from the forces' married quarters, so it was difficult for mothers to have much input into playgroup life.

Playgroup accommodation was provided free in whatever premises were available on the base, so its suitability varied from place to place and although the use of the premises was free, in some cases expensive insurance was required. On the plus side the premises were frequently not used for any other purpose so the playgroup equipment could be left in place.

Life in the services could be very difficult for young wives because of a loss of personal identity. Not only was housing provided, but also all the furniture, household equipment and soft furnishings. All Army furniture etc had to be accounted for when the regiment moved on and any damage or breakages paid for. Quarters were rigorously scrutinised to ensure they were clean enough for the next tenants to occupy. This could cause considerable stress to mothers with two or three under-fives. All mail, and even library tickets, came to the husband's place of work. Few services houses had personal phones and there were no mobile phones. Transport was very limited and only a few wives had access to cars.

Playgroups often met five days a week. Children might be taken from two and a half years and the adult:child ratio required by the forces was one adult to ten children compared with one to eight or one to six in civilian playgroups. To give an idea of the numbers involved: in 1977 in Wiltshire there were nearly 1,000 children in forces playgroups. In 1988, there were over 15,000 under-fives on service bases in Germany.

Locally, branches and counties identified forces groups in their areas and did their best to provide support. It was not always easy due to the nature of services life: regiments moved lock, stock and barrel every two years; many bases were in isolated areas with little access to transport. However, PPA courses were appreciated as were branch bulk-buying services and access to toy libraries.

There had been informal contacts with PPA national adviser Brenda Crowe in the 70s and this led in 1980 to a formal invitation from the Army to PPA to send two representatives to visit playgroups in Germany. The chairman of the National Executive Committee (NEC) and the national adviser with responsibility for forces playgroups spent a week visiting playgroups from Fallingbostel to Rheindahlen. They were welcomed by many playgroups and met people involved with playgroups – from cleaners to garrison commanders, from SSAFA Sisters* to Education Officers and, of course, many mothers, playgroup leaders and children. This visit laid the foundation for future PPA developments in Germany.

> Everywhere we went we were greatly struck by the enthusiasm of the people we met, by their feelings of isolation from the United Kingdom and their almost desperate desire for identity in their work. (National Adviser Report, 1980)

In spite of the problems presented by travelling long distances, the barriers of the rank system and the lack of personal identity experienced by forces wives, people travelled great distances to talk to the PPA representatives and join in the informal sessions. One mother attending a third session said, ' I just can't get enough of PPA'. Four indomitable playgroup mothers endured an eighteen-hour journey from Berlin on the sealed train through East Germany to join their colleagues in the British sector and then had to make the return journey the following day.

While mothers welcomed the opportunity to be involved in PPA, it was necessary to persuade the military bureaucracy that PPA had something to offer also to the British Forces in Germany. At the end of the week the PPA representatives were invited to report back to senior officers and five areas for development in Germany were identified:

1. *Access to the same PPA training opportunities and courses in Germany as in the UK*
   Agreed methods were: PPA help for people wishing to set up courses in Germany; people with BFPO addresses to be accepted on the Open University's *Pre-school Child* course; PPA provision of tutors for regular training sessions on adult learning skills, travel and accommodation to be provided by the Army; an annual playgroup conference in Germany for which PPA would provide speakers.

2. *Development in Germany of PPA branches*
   These could organise courses and develop services such as bulk-buying and toy libraries.

3. *Mother and toddler groups*
   This development was hindered by uncertainty about the insurance position for mothers using services buses, but PPA was happy to provide support and many SSAFA Sisters, seeing the benefits for young mothers, were willing to offer help.

---

* In Germany SSAFA (Soldiers, Sailors and Air Force Families Association) Sisters not only acted as health visitors but were also involved in providing personal support to young mothers. Their commitment to confidentiality was highly valued.

4. *Parental involvement*

   This was not commonly found in forces playgroups, but there was great enthusiasm to develop along these lines and the development would be facilitated if the Army supported and promoted it.

5. *Support for playgroups and parents with children with disabilities*

   PPA was willing to provide support and appropriate contacts.

Over the next few years there were several high level meetings with services personnel both in Germany and in London. PPA must have been very challenging to them but they were unfailingly polite and welcoming to PPA's representatives. Invaluable allies in the cause were SSAFA and officers from the British Forces Education Services. Both these agencies were convinced of the value of parental involvement to the health and wellbeing of young families.

PPA development in Germany was very rapid. The first branch was formed in 1980 and three more by 1983. By 1988 there was a full-time PPA Co-ordinator in Germany funded by the Ministry of Defence. She rapidly realised how impossible it would be to cover an area the size of Wales single-handed; the MoD agreed to fund four area organisers to work across British Forces in Germany. PPA courses became widely available throughout the Armed Forces in Germany.

The total spin-offs from all the PPA involvement with the services would be impossible to catalogue, but a few highlights stay in the mind:

> After seeing mothers from Army, Navy and Air Force playgroups who had not met before get together on a playgroup course, the RAF Education Officer on Gibraltar said, 'I have never had the centre so full of women having such a good time, making so much noise and learning so much.'

> A CO's wife in Germany commented, 'I really feel for these young mothers and want to help but it's so difficult for them to accept me. Perhaps helping at the playgroup is the way to do it.'

> The driver who drove the PPA representatives round Germany and humped the boxes in and out of the car had a private request: 'I never knew little kids could use paint. Can I have some for my wife to try?'

> A shrewd garrison commander in Wiltshire observed, 'If the wives are happier we will have happier soldiers.' (National Adviser Reports, 1980-83)

In parallel with developments in Germany, an Armed Forces Group (AFG) was set up by PPA in the UK. Its origin was the identification of the needs of under- fives and their families on forces bases in the UK.

The chair of the Armed Forces Group said in 1988:

> These groups are ever changing and ever moving as new commands come in
> and others leave. Nothing is constant. It takes some getting used to if you are
> continually being moved not only from house to house, or even town to town,
> but country to country. These families have to cope with constant uprooting.

The AFG provided support to all forces member groups and supported fieldworkers working with services playgroups in the UK and overseas. There were
services playgroups in Gibraltar, Cyprus, Nepal and Hong Kong. In Hong
Kong they joined the PPA branch, which also had civilian members.

Teenagers

During the 1970s a new and different kind of community support became
necessary when education for parenthood was included in the secondary
school curriculum. As a result of this, PPA groups throughout the country
found they were being approached to provide school pupils with experience
relevant to work with under-fives. This sometimes took the form of a contribution to a home economics course and on other occasions formed part of a
community development project. It very soon became obvious that adequate
preparation and planning were essential if the experience was to be a valuable one for both the teens and the groups concerned.

PPA responded to the challenge and developed guidelines, produced leaflets
and organised local conferences to consider the issues. These included
whether placements were appropriate for the group concerned; how to ensure
that any involvement of teenagers did not detract from the needs of the playgroup families; how to provide adequate preparation for both the group and
the pupils; how to ensure that parent involvement was unaffected; and how
costs were to be met.

There was much learning by all concerned. Adults in both schools and playgroups came to recognise that:

- ☐ Teenagers who had had inadequate play experience as children
  needed to make up the deficit before they could look outwards to the
  needs of the children. This could be addressed by providing opportunities to visit the playgroup with no children present so that the
  teenagers could experiment with the play material and learn why
  such equipment was provided.
- ☐ The playgroup experience led to huge growth in self-esteem in some
  teenagers who were now for the first time in their lives seen by

younger children as a source of information, support and authority. 'Pete, a walking disaster at home and in class, was everyone's favourite at playgroup ... which gave him real confidence.'

- [ ] For some teenagers it was the first time they had been made to feel useful and to be an active part of an adult working group.

- [ ] For teenagers who might be experiencing difficult relationships with parents and teachers, playgroup experience provided an opportunity to receive kindness and support from mature adults who had no preconceived ideas about them.

- [ ] For some playgroup mothers it was an opportunity to break down barriers with teenagers whom they had previously perceived as threatening.

Some teachers initially considered that playgroup experience was less relevant to the more academic teenagers. It was pointed out that those aspiring to higher education can also grow into parents, and the ability to relate to children and understand their needs is surely an essential life skill.

Schools were also unwilling occasionally to send boys, on the grounds that such experience was not important for them. Playgroup people, however, welcomed both boys and girls, not just because boys might some day be fathers, but because in an age when boys are expected to be tough there may be few opportunities for them to develop their natural potential for gentleness and sensitivity. They could also provide useful role models for boys in the playgroup, especially those with no father at home.

The learning from these experiences continued after the placements, and many teenagers became actively involved with parents or the group itself after they left. This happened in many different ways. Some became babysitters for families they had met; others arranged playgroup parties, helped with playgroup outings or became involved in fundraising for the group.

Everyone involved learned a great deal in the process. A secondary teacher writing to thank her local group said:

> We all realise how much extra work and planning it means to have teens present, but for them it is an experience of inestimable value ... We hope ... that this will encourage more thoughtful relationships between our teens, their own friends and their parents as well as with younger children. (PPA *Welcoming Teenagers into PPA Groups*, 1983:6)

A teenaged girl expressed similar thoughts:

> I think that going to playgroup helps you learn about children better than books
> ... you learn how to get on with young children ... and have more fun with them
> than reading about them. (*ibid*:6)

Welcoming Teenagers into PPA Groups also pointed out that:

> Many groups have handicapped children and it is a valuable experience for
> young people to get to know them as part of a family in the community. They
> begin to understand how to help in a positive way rather than reacting with fear
> or too much sympathy. (*ibid*:9)

In 1977, in response to growing numbers of unemployed people, the Manpower Services Commission was set up to run public employment and training services. With high numbers of unemployed teenagers, PPA groups were an obvious resource and the experience gained from working with teenagers from schools and colleges proved invaluable for PPA people coping with this new challenge. In some areas MSC involvement was a very positive experience; in others it was less so, particularly if the organisers were unwilling to work with the existing provision. The growth of government-sponsored schemes for under-fives (20,000 pre-school children were involved in 1987 alone) led to PPA's collaboration with other agencies in producing a report on the subject. This made recommendations to the government about ensuring that MSC schemes should not overlap with or detract from existing voluntary provision.

Community service orders

Occasionally, teenagers arrived in playgroups from a different direction. In some areas well-screened young offenders who had been given community service sentences by the courts completed some of their unpaid work hours in playgroups. They benefited from the opportunity to make a positive contribution in a supportive setting, among adults who were sympathetic while still demanding the high standards required of anybody working with young children. These initiatives involved a great deal of preparation and discussion, both with the Probation Service to provide necessary reassurance for parents and staff, and also within the playgroups concerned to ensure the necessary balance was maintained between the needs of the teenagers and those of the playgroup children and their families.

Fathers

PPA groups also brought challenges and opportunities for fathers through their families' involvement in PPA groups. For some fathers the desire for a closer involvement may have been triggered by attendance at one of the National Childbirth Trust's antenatal classes, which were growing in popularity in the 80s. For others it grew from the experiences of their wives, partners and children who were sharing new experiences in playgroups and wanted to involve fathers in the same venture. There was a growing awareness of the role of fathers with their children due, in part, to the work of PPA.

Some PPA groups organised special sessions for fathers so that they too could learn about the pleasures of playing with sand and water, mess about with paint and create elaborate constructions with building blocks. Many were also able to contribute their skills to playgroup sessions, perhaps by playing a musical instrument, demonstrating sporting skills, engaging in craft activities or turning their hands to practical tasks such as repairs to the buildings and equipment used by the playgroup.

Innumerable fathers also shared in the administrative work of playgroups, perhaps by serving on the committee or providing useful contacts for fundraising.

For househusbands or single fathers, involvement in a PPA group could bring companionship and support as well as giving them a chance to be popular role models for the children in the group.

For some fathers, their wives' playgroup involvement could sometimes feel puzzling, and even threatening. A PPA tutor recalls:

> I remember that some husbands refused to let their wives go on courses, fearful that they would fly (in both senses), going too far, getting qualifications, going to college, leaving home, getting ideas, etc.

For many more fathers, however, the energy and commitment their playgroup wives brought back into the home was a shared asset. Many men even caught the volunteering habit and stayed involved with their children as they moved on:

> When our boys left the playgroup I started to help at the Cubs and became a leader. It seemed the natural thing to do, and now my grandchildren come too. (Playgroup father, personal letter)

Grandparents

It was obvious that grandparents who lived locally could become involved in the playgroup with their grandchildren. Many were the prime carers for the grandchildren while the parents were working. In some communities this had long been the traditional role of grandparents. But the extended family was breaking down. The reality for many young families was living on an isolated housing estate far from the nearest town or, even worse, in a bleak tower block with friends and family far away. In these circumstances many young women endured a lonely daily life with their young children, having little access to any respite, transport or friends, and without the support and advice that their own parents might once have been around to offer.

In these circumstances, older people welcomed into the playgroup as helpers could and often did become surrogate grandparents. This provided a valuable asset within the group and also eased the pain for grandparents who were prevented by distance or divorce from seeing their own grandchildren:

> Helping at playgroup helped to keep me sane when my daughter and my grandchildren went to live in Australia. (Personal letter)

> I've always loved young children but couldn't have any; now I feel fulfilled by being a playgroup grandmother. (Playgroup helper, 1975)

Families in socially disadvantaged areas

Seeking ways to break the 'cycle of deprivation', government minister Keith Joseph in 1972 described the playgroup movement as 'a necessary social service, not a substitute educational one'. One of the recommendations of Lord Scarman's (1981) report into the Brixton riots was the need for more playgroups. In some places, PPA groups reached out to more socially disadvantaged and inner city local communities, offering hope in the face of very serious social problems. This help was also extended to isolated pockets of deprivation in otherwise more affluent areas.

In London, Inner London PPA (Hanton, 1977) supported the development of over 400 under-five groups, often providing a 'child-centred oasis in a concrete wilderness'. In addition to playgroups there were drop-ins, parent-toddler groups, family playgroups (with grandparents and teenagers welcome), one o'clock clubs meeting in city parks, playbuses, crèches, language groups for non-English-speaking mothers, and some day care and extended day playgroups. Most play leaders lived within walking distance and were not previously professionally trained but had attended a PPA Foundation Course. There was a strong supportive network of advisers, peripatetic play leaders, course tutors and committees, and good working relationships with local authorities, especially social services and adult education. Together they provided the skilled leadership and professional backing that an early National Children's Bureau study (Ferri, 1977) showed to be necessary for groups to succeed in social priority areas. Government, and trust grants supported the work.

Sometimes the spur came from an unlooked-for source. The Bunbury Project was named after Miss E. Bunbury, who left money, 'for the benefit of children preferably in a group activity with adults'. Approached by Dr John Bowlby for ideas on how to meet Miss Bunbury's wishes, Inner London PPA (ILPPA) initially suggested a playgroup for minded children and their carers; child-minding was at that time a much neglected and maligned form of childcare. Childminders, when asked, said they wanted something free and informal without a commitment to regular attendance. They recognised their respon-sibility for the children, but wanted a break – a cup of tea, a chat, a smoke – whilst somebody else kept them occupied. Clearly not a playgroup. Never-theless, after much deliberation, it was decided to go along with the idea of a free drop in and to provide high quality play for the children together with support in the home. The underlying principles and values remained those of PPA playgroups – trust, inclusiveness and openness, putting children and families first, plus deepening understanding of how people learn and grow.

In 1975, the first informal drop-in for childminders began; it offered a place for childminders to meet, together with opportunities to observe different ways of responding to children and to experiment with a variety of inexpen-sive play activities that they could try out at home (Shinman, 1979). Over time, childminders decided not to smoke when caring for children; they began enjoying play with them in the group setting, becoming increasingly sensitive to their needs and keen on training further (Shinman in Evans, 2000).

The idea flourished and expanded because of the co-operation between the Trustees of the Bunbury legacy, ILPPA, Lewisham PPA, the project workers and Lewisham Borough, and their willingness, in line with the PPA ethos in which the scheme was rooted, to work with rather than for childminders.

Across the country, experienced PPA people were setting up local projects to reach socially disadvantaged families, although sadly this was not nationally documented or publicised. By 1980, one in ten PPA groups was in an inner city area. (PPA Facts and Figures, 1980). For example, in Portsmouth Docks a PPA adviser worked with mothers who were prostitutes, as well as organising places for over 1,000 under-fives and setting up informal courses (*Contact*, March 1973). A Carnegie Trust grant in the early 1980s enabled Gateshead PPA branch to set up a free parent and toddler club in an inner-city area of high unemployment. This was so successful that the parents themselves set up and ran a second session. The wider Cheshire project (Palfreeman and Smith, 1982) began in 1973, as its PPA co-ordinator relates:

> The PPA area organiser asked me to help her to advise a church group in a very deprived area. This experience convinced me that with support such groups could work. (I asked) the social services director ... if he would fund us to set up playgroups in deprived areas – which he did. At first we were told constantly it would not work and we often felt vulnerable and isolated. However, the director of education ... was impressed by what we were achieving; he offered me a desk with clerical support. Project leaders and I found skills we didn't know we had.

So did the mothers (see chapter 2). Mothers in the most deprived areas had a hunger for knowledge and playgroup leaders in poor areas went on to become elected councillors and magistrates, take O and A levels and gain various professional qualifications.

The Cheshire project was largely community development work. It was 'slow and painstaking work to get to know an area and its possibilities and to make local contacts in building a new group.' Also it was not enough to help set up a group. Groups experienced recurring change and crises, and it 'needed constant effort to create, and then to maintain, people's confidence in their own abilities' (Palfreeman and Smith, 1982:20). That it was often successful is reflected in local authority awareness of things happening differently and parents who now talked about wanting to do things.

Family centres

Some of the first projects to reach disadvantaged families were family centres. Scottish PPA's Stepping Stone Projects, reflecting on their first years of work (1978-81) in the most socially deprived neighbourhoods, found that a family centre offering a range of activities and a community development approach was easier to sustain, in terms of volunteer and professional support and grant aid, than smaller one-off projects (Overton, 1981).

As it became apparent that this approach was effective, a patchwork of funding and co-operation emerged involving a range of statutory and voluntary agencies and funding sources. For example, a local PPA branch began work in 1982 in a dockside estate, where half the mothers were single parents and most families were on benefits. As the initiative developed, it gained support from the government's Opportunities for Volunteering scheme through PPA. Later, an Urban Aid application was successful. Starting with a playgroup and mother-toddler group, it grew to become Marsh Lane Family Centre, with a wide range of additional activities: a toy library, home visiting, welfare rights and family planning advice, a parents' lunch club, courses and activities for parents (including parenting courses), a drop-in and crisis support for families, drugs counselling, an after-school play club, a mini-youth club for 5-7 year olds, a summer playscheme, and even a seaside holiday for a group of families. There was close liaison with local agencies, including regular working lunch meetings. Parents were fully involved in running the centre, which took pride in being flexible enough to respond to the changing needs of families (PPA Acorn Committee Report, 1988, based on 150 completed questionnaires). The approach was practical, based on helping parents grow in skills and confidence, to the advantage of both their children and themselves. However, the underlying way of working was not spelled out as deliberately as in the Scottish Stepping Stone Projects.

The Stepping Stone Project Report explained the common features of their family centres. The primary task was to provide a positive environment for parents and children, above all a secure base (Winnicott's and Bowlby's ideas provide the underpinning theory), enabling parents to help themselves:

> Our hopes, and indeed our growing belief, is that it is possible at this early stage of relationships between parent and child to create a kind of 'second chance'. Although nothing can remove the bad experiences that a mother or father may have had in their own childhood, if there is a time of catching up, of having good experiences for oneself as for one's child, within a supportive and small group setting, then some of the early damage may be repaired ....

> It is only when there are some signs of 'recovery' by the parents that they become genuinely able to respond more positively to the demands of their toddlers. This is perhaps the reason why no amount of advice, however wisely and kindly given, by 'those who know' has the lasting effect we think it should. The mysterious processes of being 'good enough' parents depend on the parents' own inner resources and state of mind. (Overton, 1981)

Activities grew out of parents' and leaders' ideas, working together with the aim of parents feeling involved and responsible. This was a long-term process and could not be hurried; it could take months.

A weekly users' meeting (open to all, although a management committee with limited membership might provide support) was one place where plans were made and decisions taken. This gave parents real responsibility; it is all too easy for dependency and then apathy to build around over-directive leadership. The meeting allowed people to express strong feelings, often anger. Success was about trusting in the process of expressing and working through feelings in an emotionally containing group, rather than solving people's problems for them. At first the leader provided the holding until parents learned to do it for themselves. The help parents were able to give to one another was often the most acceptable, but it took time to reach this point:

> We undertake a continuous debate about the nature of the balance of respon-
> sibilities between the families in the projects and the workers. On the one hand
> project workers are continuously seeking ways in which responsibilities and
> decision taking can be shared; on the other hand, if this is taken too fast, there
> is confusion, lack of understanding and the eventual fall away of the families
> concerned. There are dangers of both going too fast and being over-protective,
> and the balance seems never to be resolved. (*ibid*:3)

In turn, there was recognition of leaders' needs for organised and active support, supervision and funding.

Although articulated most clearly in Scotland, this way of working reflected what was happening in many PPA-inspired family centres across the country (McMahon and Ward, 2001). These family centres were the precursors to the early Sure Start children's centre programmes which began, many in existing family centres, in areas of greatest deprivation, and which initially sought to empower small groups of parents to make the major decisions about what they wanted of early years provision in their neighbourhood. This proved to be slow work; parents need time to develop the necessary skills and self-confidence. It can be frustrating for some professionals who have to learn not to impose what they think would be best, to build parents' self-confidence until they are able to articulate what they actually want as opposed to what others tell them they need, and to live with parents' decisions which they sometimes feel are not well advised. Playgroup people knew and know that this sort of change cannot be achieved instantly – we lived it ourselves.

'Families who can't become families who do'

This quotation comes from a report on PPA's involvement in the Opportunities for Volunteering Initiative during the 1980s when PPA was recognised as a credible national organisation that could deliver targeted government funding in areas of need. Grants were given for family drop-in centres, hospital play schemes and schemes to help children with disabilities. Between 1982 and 1989 PPA allocated £650,000 to 105 such groups in many parts of the country.

One project that benefited was set up to provide support for families with a child who had special needs. A later report indicated that the drop-in centre established for this purpose had grown into an integral part of a family therapy clinic, used and respected by all concerned.

Family centres were locally based, usually in deprived areas, open to all families with under-fives and offering a range of services. Mothers talking about their local centre said:

> Everyone helps with everyone else's kid. It's a great place. My family has gained happiness and that is plenty to what we had before.

> To me a centre such as this is vital to families, the community, and probably to the future of our children. (Barbara Clarke on OMEP Conference, 1989: *The Voice of the Child*)

Co-operation within the community

Useful contacts developed with local primary schools often led to liaison between reception teachers and playgroups so that the teacher could visit the playgroup, and playgroup children ready for school could visit the school before they started. These links increased mutual understanding and often made transitions easier, as both children and parents had become comfortable in the school environment before the child left playgroup. Teachers, likewise, found it easier to arrange appropriate programmes of learning for children whom they had been able to observe informally during visits to the playgroup.

There was one interesting spin-off from the setting up of a playgroup in a rapidly growing village with a very large number of under-fives. The playgroup committee were quick to realise that the two existing schools would not be able to cope with the numbers, so they worked with the local Residents' Association to organise a door-to-door survey of under-fives. The short-term outcome was more recruits for the playgroup, which opened more sessions. The long-term result was a new school for the village. One mother recalling the campaigning said, 'I remember going from door to door with a baby on my back and a toddler in the buggy.'

The integration of the playgroup, once seen as a usurper, into the structure of local communities gave PPA people a stronger voice and also provided them with useful contacts, enabling them to extend their work when need and opportunity arose.

And extend it they did. From Educational Priority Areas to local playbuses, from play schemes for children with special needs to work in women's refuges, where there were families and young children in need of support, the energy, initiative and innovative determination of PPA volunteers, working within organisational structures that left them free to respond and initiate at local level, transformed the lives of individuals and communities.

PPA's report to the Department of Health in 1989 said:

> Projects thrive where there is a high standard of co-operation within a community between all the relevant agencies ... this pooling of resources pays dividends ... Families who at first can't, become families who do, and go on to help other families develop likewise.

5

Moving on – the policy, process and outcomes

Sheila Shinman

The Pre-school Playgroups Association (PPA) wrote a Moving On policy into the constitution for the national body and for its member playgroups. This system put a three or, at the most, a six-year ceiling on the time spent in any committee role (but not on staff roles such as play leader, supervisor or national staff member). The Association intended to ensure that each successive group of parents, with their children in a playgroup, would all have opportunities to develop new skills. One committee member described it as, 'A year to find out about the role and learn it, a year to consolidate and make a difference, and a year to find a successor.'

All policies have their strengths, weaknesses and, sometimes, unintended consequences. 'Moving on', as argued in other chapters, is no exception. On the plus side, it is widely seen as having enabled mothers to participate in the excitement, creativity and idealism of the movement and as having kept those qualities alive for succeeding generations of parents. In so doing, it changed the lives of significant numbers of women from a wide range of backgrounds by helping them to progress through the organisation, to widen horizons, to gain skills and to go on and do things they had never dreamed of, both in PPA and beyond.

All this was felt worthy of investigation. Accordingly, a pilot enquiry (see p173) was carried out into how parents feel now about their participation in PPA and playgroups, and what it has meant to them personally and to their families. What follows tells how some who lived through the first three decades of the process, many of whom are now grandparents, look back on their experiences then and later. It examines how these experiences fitted into the political and social background of the time and whether any aspects of the policy may be relevant to young families and early years policies today.

Who responded?

In spite of a short timescale, few resources, and the difficulties of finding people 50 years on, 134 people who were once active members of PPA (a response rate of 70%) returned questionnaires. Respondents came from all regions of Great Britain, but disappointingly few from Wales. Perhaps this was because we had few contacts, and Welsh members may have felt that they had already contributed to a national record of their experiences (Bray *et al* (eds), 2008).

Of the 100 people who met the deadline for replies, there was one man; the rest were women, two of whom had no children. Thirty-seven had joined a playgroup in the 1960s, 44 in the 70s and nine in the 80s; ten did not say. Respondents described more playgroups in towns, villages and rural areas than cities. A picture emerged of mainly young mothers, well over a third of whom had recently moved away from family and friends, a few coming from Europe, from army garrisons, and from as far away as Australia, Canada and Papua New Guinea, to live in unfamiliar surroundings, on new estates or villages. Some were expecting their first child, others had several under-fives, and a very few had teenage children as well. A high proportion of mothers, especially in rural areas (33 out of 56 respondents), said they had done voluntary work before playgroup involvement, mainly through the church, but many others spoke of feeling lonely and isolated.

The process
Initiative takers

Comprehensive information was lacking about parents' occupations before they started a family, but it was clear that many of the 28 people who took the initiative in starting a playgroup had been university graduates, civil servants, teachers, nursery nurses or nurses or a combination of these. Some began their playgroup in the home as a tentative experiment, perhaps with a friend. Others brought friends and neighbours together to discuss the idea and take it forward; others yet again started up on their own initiative, but employed a qualified play leader. In the early days, this process was extremely informal. Later, more structured approaches and formal qualifications were required.

Getting involved

Most mothers had heard about playgroups by word of mouth. A very few said they saw a notice in the village shop or received a mail drop, whilst health visitors recommended others to a local playgroup. Only two mothers cited Belle Tutaev's letter to *The Guardian* as the trigger to starting a playgroup.

Most of those who said they had worked before marriage gave it up to be at home once they started a family. It was the norm. Many felt a lack of company for their children and for themselves. Some took their children first to private nurseries; others were initially wary of playgroups as being a less good form of provision.

A house move that led to joining a new group, a change in play leader, or both, were often catalysts for changed attitudes towards active participation in a group. As one mother wrote:

> Would I ever have got involved if I hadn't moved house – away from a private group to a village with a mother and toddler group and to a playgroup well established in the community?

Indeed the play leader emerges as gatekeeper to parent involvement in the playgroup, and some mothers said that it took several playgroups or nurseries before they found one in which they could be involved.

Mothers from a range of social and educational backgrounds all eventually found themselves on parent rotas, part of a community of people who cared about their children but who possibly knew very little about child development and were unsure about childcare:

> Despite a degree and a postgraduate diploma in education I felt totally incompetent and didn't have a clue as to how to cope with a baby or small child.

They said they were there initially because they recognised their children's, and sometimes their own, need for companionship. The possibility of doing something about it themselves began to dawn, and to inspire and galvanise them into action.

Every mother, unless she had a very young child, was expected to take a turn helping in the playgroup. Parents describe some rotas as haphazard, others as highly organised with teams and leaders. Responsibilities often extended to raising funds, committee work, washing up and helping with setting out and tidying up equipment, as well as playing with the children. Fathers, and often the whole family, were involved. Moreover, it was fun! Whatever they did, mothers recall this period of involvement as a very happy time.

Deepening participation and the emergence of themes

What hooked (a word that recurs) a person into deeper involvement seems to have been the warmth, commitment and quality of relationships between group members. Parents refer to the excitement of finding themselves with other like-minded people, the sense of being part of something worthwhile, of learning and achievement, and of making a difference – whether in the playgroup, at a branch meeting or inspired by speakers at annual general meetings and national conferences:

> ... went to the Bristol 1968 conference – was hooked ...

> I was overwhelmed by the sense of being part of a shared vision – a huge group of people who cared about the same things as me.

Intertwining pathways

From this point, 'moving on' offered a variety of pathways for mothers whose energy, imagination, creativity and abilities had often been limited by an un-fulfilling experience of school or by the home environment, or who had cut short stimulating work experience to start a family, and felt the loss.

Most of these pathways followed on in sequential tiers of responsibility within the organisation. This was 'moving on'. Starting in the playgroup, there was en-couragement to attend branch meetings. The next progression was to county and regional levels, first as a representative on a committee, with the oppor-tunity of a stint as chair, probably with a spell as area organiser and under-taking some tutoring on the way. The next step might be to become a regional representative on one of the national subcommittees. Not everyone enjoyed moving on through every tier, but the chance to have a go was invaluable in finding out what felt good and sometimes led in surprising directions:

> It taught me what I do well (organising events, writing for *Contact*) and what I don't do well. No one will ever persuade me to chair anything again.

Several of these pathways overlap, intersect or run parallel, but when mapped are clearly discernible. They show the routes whereby opportunities to 'taste' and contribute in different ways to the group's purposes interacted with a person's hitherto unrecognised abilities and desires.

They all stem from interest in the children in the playgroup, at first usually a mother's own, but soon extending to other people's children. In addition to what she learned from observing and helping in the group, there were courses she could follow, and encouragement and practical support to do so:

> I went to the AGM because I thought it was the thing to do and came away as secretary.

> You can do it!

> I was nudged into it!

As has been shown in earlier chapters, everyone can learn from each other and share experiences. If it is an enjoyable experience, it makes the time spent with children more fulfilling. One course whets the appetite for another.

Three main routes

1. When their children started school, some mothers were happy to continue working in the playgroup, either voluntarily or as a paid play leader, learning more about how best to work with the children and in their community.

2. Others found fulfilment in sharing what they were learning with others. They extended their studies and began tutoring short courses, perhaps making use of earlier studies or work experience but with a different slant:

> It did not change the way I saw teaching, but it enabled me to reflect in ways I would probably not have done.

> I already had teaching qualifications but PPA opened my eyes to how other people could develop their skills and qualifications through PPA methods and training.

Many describe developing new courses specially tailored for playgroup people. It was exciting and stimulating. Mothers grew through the organisation from becoming area organisers[1] to tutoring the Foundation Course, to engaging in fieldwork, to arranging courses through local colleges and universities, including distance learning through the Open University. Seven stayed in the movement as training and development officers and four became national advisers.

3. Satisfaction and fulfilment for others lay in the organisational and business aspects of PPA: obtaining what the group needed by negotiating over premises or with the local authority or the media. PPA members ensured funding, accounted for how it was used and spread the message about what was being done and what was needed. Perhaps a committee member, hesitant and feeling incapable, found, with encouragement from someone who was moving on, that they had ideas, skills and abilities that were valued by the group. Even a chance possession could lead to unexpected developments. One mother told how a birthday present of a calculator (uncommon in those early days) led her to accept the unlooked-for role of treasurer. Others took on

the role of chair and all, like the children, were learning by doing. Each had the opportunity, as committee member, minute taker, chair or treasurer, to develop that role in the context of the PPA branch, county or region and at national level.

There were other pathways that met the needs of both the individual and the groups as they developed. There were initiatives such as bulk-buying – a boon for many playgroups, particularly those in villages who could not easily get to town to find the products that they needed. As described in chapter 4, other initiatives reached out to engage with teenagers in playgroups, playbuses for Travellers, support for prisoners' families, organising events, fundraising in the playgroups, running conferences and AGMs.

These patterns and intertwining pathways, themes with variations, run through all responses.

Fifty years later, how do mothers judge their experiences in playgroups and in PPA?

> It's all so long ago.
>
> Perhaps I'm looking through a rosy glow.
>
> I can't remember the dates, but ...

It's a big but.

Experiences at playgroup level: the pros

Mothers often couch positive aspects of playgroups and PPA in personal and highly emotional terms. The overwhelming response to the experience in the playgroups with the children is positive and joyous:

> It was the happiest time of my life.

'Happy' is the word that appears most often to describe the time in the play-group. Happiness and fun qualify as major themes. They centre on emotions, enjoyment and personal benefits:

> There were the home corner, painted orange boxes for cooker, cots made from tomato boxes, home-made play foods, salt dough, clothes horses hanging dressing-up clothes, books, cushions, puzzles, soft toys, painting.

> I remember great fundraising social evenings, cheese and wine, Tupperware, jewellery and clothes parties. What fun!

> Let's all have fun together. We can do it and do it better. We can all learn to-gether.

But learning what? Doing what? Child development, how to play with children and how to manage difficult behaviour, a better understanding of children's needs through careful observation, ideas for play to take home... One mother summed it up:

It completely changed how I parented my children. I enjoyed being a parent.

Another saw it this way:

In PPA I learned that people learn by doing and not by being talked at, that learning is lifelong, that people learn best in informal settings.

Through doing it themselves and together, mothers began to develop a belief in their own and others' ability to achieve something positive for their children, and then realised how they themselves were benefiting:

I learned that there are many ways of learning, and that people with a non-academic background can be as capable as me.

Mothers refer to general changes in outlook: that working together was more effective than going it alone, that they began to see problems as challenges, that they could still be friends with people who had different ideas from theirs and, for many, the realisation (and relief) that they did not need paper qualifications to be there.

Two mothers wrote:

I learned to organise work well, and not to conclude that people of differing opinions are either idiots or villains.

Everyone has something to offer. Volunteers come in all shapes and sizes.

The two themes, fun and learning, worked together in positive ways. The very process of learning in a happy, creative environment, open to all, bred confidence – another major theme:

I've been thirsty for information ever since ... I probably always had the ability, but never the belief in myself at that stage in life. PPA gave me the confidence to achieve all that I have in the educational field.

Making friends began in the playgroup and carried on at all levels. Seventy-five out of a 100 mothers refer to the importance of friendship:

When we meet it's as though time has stood still and we pick up as though we were together only yesterday.

Lifelong friendships were forged not just between individuals but also between networks of women living in the same locality. Such groups still meet within the regions. They are not backward looking and nostalgic; members say that much as they enjoyed PPA, they seldom talk about the old days; they are too busy doing new things.

Experiences at playgroup level: the cons
These turn out to be mainly environmental, physical and social. Whilst most mothers found they could think only of advantages, some remember disadvantages. Clearly recalled are problems relating to premises – cold church halls and the hard physical task and mindless chore of humping equipment out from storage (often under a stage), setting it out in advance of opening time and putting it all back again afterwards.

A few playgroup leaders and committee members recall that not all church members, proprietors or caretakers were happy about laying their premises open to activities that included sand and water play, dough, paint, Plasticine and the like. Mothers needed to explain and negotiate; and even some of the shyest found that, for the children and the playgroup, they could stand up and argue for their convictions.

The very early days are not all remembered as carefree. Not all professionals, especially health visitors and teachers, thought playgroups were a good idea; some could be obstructive. In addition, as the responsibilities of running a playgroup grew, with new laws requiring contracts of employment, tensions arising from employing staff and handling money sometimes became destructive:

> We made a lot of mistakes. It wasn't all sweetness and light.

Play leaders sometimes found it difficult to involve all the parents in ways they wished:

> Some people didn't want to join in and some who wanted to join in wanted to rule the roost.

This could stem from the mothers' expectation that they could leave their children and have some time for themselves – respite care! It could also be a question of money, and mothers wanting or needing to work – for example in playgroups run for army families. When forces husbands were away for long periods, wives often wanted to work and therefore sought a different kind of childcare. Traditional playgroups did not meet the needs of every child and parent.

Whether playgroups were experienced as a pro or a con, one overwhelming outcome turned out to be increasing confidence in abilities, feelings of emotional and intellectual fulfilment, of challenges met:

> Playgroup was my jumping-off point.

But to what?

Increasing participation, increasing gains and losses

As participation at different levels of the movement grew, calls on officers' and committee members' time increased. Travel often played a significant part in their lives. This was, on one hand, a source of great satisfaction. It involved meeting new people, stimulating and informative discussion and negotiation, learning and sharing, a sometimes intoxicating sense of achievement:

> We felt we were changing the world for the under-fives.

On the other hand, it could also mean lengthy periods away from home, long days travelling by train ('interminable'), or by car ('honed geographical and navigational skills'- no satnavs then) – and late nights. Looking back, some mothers wonder how good this was for some of their children – particularly the youngest. Older children soon cottoned on:

> A young daughter was heard crying, ' Mummy! Mummy!' while her older sister advised, 'Call her Mrs T, like in playgroup, then she'll come.'

Telephones were in a sense the arteries and lifeblood of the organisation. They enabled members to inform and support each other, confer, discuss, come to decisions, let off steam.

Telephones also rang frequently – at meal times, when you were in the bath (no cordless phones or mobiles in those days), relaxing or at other inconvenient times:

> ... including when I was giving birth at home to my fourth child.

Although some children learned to be very efficient secretaries, such pressures caused ructions in many families. Spoilt or late meals, expensive telephone bills and car usage, especially when there was only one breadwinner and in periods of recession, could cause damaging tension. Husbands did not always see the value of volunteering – it was 'not a proper job'. Some marriages broke up under the strain as, at the same time, wives perhaps outgrew their husbands or husbands could not tolerate what they saw as dereliction of wifely duties. Few of our respondents reported personal break-ups, but most knew they happened. Those involved probably include parents who did not participate in the enquiry.

Those who did respond were far more likely to tell of benefits arising from changed relationships, and of advantages for the whole family by participating in playgroup activities. Many husbands were supportive. They made and repaired toys and helped with moving heavy equipment. They cooked meals and even 'supplied coffee and biscuits for groups of chattering women and cleared up afterwards'.

One small but observant daughter, when asked at school what her parents did, wrote:

> Daddy does the washing, he does the hoovering, and he makes the beds. Mummy goes to playgroup.

Husbands stepped in and looked after children, allowing their wives to go off to residential courses or conferences. Several mothers remarked that this hands-on support, unusual in fathers at the time, strengthened father-child relationships.

Other mothers insisted that their activities and commitment to the playgroup movement gave them an interest outside the home that they could combine with being at home with the children when it mattered. It gave them something to talk about that helped or even saved their marriage. Overall, the family stood to benefit because mothers felt happy and fulfilled.

As with any experience – a holiday, a trauma, a job or involvement in any undertaking – memories tend to kaleidoscope and we recall 'it' as good or bad or not worth remembering. If that is true, then the overall verdict of the experience of the playgroup movement by those who replied was of a life-affirming experience.

Values and ethos

So what was it (indeed, was there an 'it'?) that playgroup people came to value so much that they were eager to record it?

This is where some differences emerge between those who continued working in playgroups as supervisors (some for twenty or thirty years) and those who moved on through the organisation to chair, to tutor and to play other parts at branch, county, regional and national levels, and who also spent several decades doing it. 'Moving on' did not limit a person to six years in the movement as a whole.

What did parents value?

A small minority of mothers did not comment on values. The majority clearly accepted more and more responsibility and threw themselves into whatever tasks and challenges came up, continuing to grow in various capacities through the movement. Thirty mothers stayed and 'moved on' for up to ten years and over half (53) for twenty and even up to thirty or more years. They are clear about what they valued, and particular values predominate in specific subgroups and in each decade.

Those who remained in the playgroups, close to children, identify values that centre on learning though play and playgroups being open to everyone, and everyone – adult and child – being valued, and able to grow at their own pace, but with every encouragement to try something new. Above all, the memories they recall revolve round fun and happy times.

Mothers who started in the 1960s, who then began to move on to branch and regional activities, also emphasise children learning through play as well as parent involvement variously expressed as:

self-help through volunteers reaching out into the community

a sense that, together we can do it

doing with, not doing for

a child-centred extended family with mothers at the heart

parents taking responsibility at every level of the organisation

fellowship and having fun together.

As people recount their deepening involvement, the value of learning through play still figures, but awareness of other factors becomes more apparent. There is an appreciation of shared adult learning, of opportunities that opened up through the movement, the encouragement to move on, to try something new and of strengthening friendships. The language changes to emphasise learning by doing. There is also growing awareness and value placed on the vision and good sense of ordinary people who don't value themselves.

One subgroup, particularly strong amongst those who started in the 1960s and 1970s, stresses the importance of mothers taking responsibility for their children's education and upbringing – not simply leaving it to experts, and not necessarily accepting the views of experts either. Parents of pre-school children see themselves as their child's best teachers, and say that playgroups run by parents provide optimum learning opportunities for all the family.

Mothers who followed the tutoring pathway tend to value the new learning that took place. Tutors comment on the rewarding ways in which many in their groups said they had never been any good at school and had nothing to offer but, through the playgroup way of learning, found they knew more than they thought, developed a lust for learning and grew. Even tutors with higher education under their belts aver how much they learned about how children and adults learn, the importance of listening, of respect, of being non-judgmental, and that everybody has something of value to offer. One mother, inspired by the PPA Foundation Course, followed it up with a Postgraduate Certificate in Education (PGCE) and commented that she had gained:

> greater understanding of how we and children learn through PPA than on the course provided by the PGCE.

Others found fulfilment through organisational and business routes. They tend to see particular value in the opportunities to experiment and to learn additional skills. Their experiences often culminated in service on one of the subcommittees of PPA's National Executive.

People who joined in the 70s share the same commitment to learning through play and to parent involvement at every level, but they are the first ones to make explicit mention of inclusiveness and equality in relation to race and special needs. New legislation (see Timeline, p179-180), the introduction of relevant courses and raised awareness of the issues were possible factors in this development. References to educating parents and benefiting children, to encouraging parents back into learning, and to the importance, or otherwise, of 'moving on' appear for the first time. There is also a feeling that, especially at regional level, 'One could get so involved that families did not come first.'

Views that are more usual, however, are of an extended family with:

> everyone taking a share in the teaching and learning that was essentially a child-centred philosophy
>
> teachers learning and learners teaching
>
> friendship, encouragement, inclusion, support, belief in people, ongoing learning, fun and hard work.

Other perspectives

Whilst most mothers comment positively about the value of the playgroup movement for them personally, several also reflect on and question other aspects.

There is overwhelming support for and appreciation of the value of PPA publications, particularly *The Business Side of Playgroups* and *Contact*. However, one respondent queries whether the wide-ranging topics covered in *Contact* really reached out to the immediate concerns of members in their playgroups:

> The PPA course gave members a far more down-to-earth grounding in good play practice and in encouraging parent involvement.

She also expresses concern about contradictions that could lead to conflict over quality assurance, and to confusion internally and externally regarding what the organisation stood for. These contradictions were between the desire for government funding and PPA's commitment to the empowerment of parents through the opportunity to take full responsibility, and between welcoming all parents and maintaining high standards of play practice for the group.

Another mother writes that PPA could have, 'taken equal opportunities work more seriously' and that 'lip service was paid.'

Some other respondents see the ethos as exclusive because the organisational structure of representation from group to branch, to county, to region to National Executive Committee (NEC) precluded the possibility of direct contact or communication between the grassroots membership and the executive in matters of policy. Others again see the structure, function and value of local meetings and national AGMs and of membership services as democracy at work.

Straws in the wind

As the movement and social conditions changed, and under the weight of increased legislation in the 80s and early 90s, there is a sense that PPA's commitment to play, something of real value, was being lost:

> I feel very sad that the organisation is no longer the driving force in the care and development of children and opportunities for parents. We live in a very changed world, but opportunities to play informally with and observe other people's children as well as our own, and learn from that, have largely been lost.

> I returned to childminding because in my role as area organiser I no longer had time to visit my groups and play with the children or meet the mums and babies. There was so much paperwork and regulations that all I ever did was to tell adults what they should do – so I left, to go back to playing. All the fun had gone.

> PPA picked me up at just the right time, when I was a young mum. It made me who I am today. I lost faith in the organisation when it changed its training to the Diploma. When I heard you could do childcare by post, it made no sense.

> The changes in PPA in the nineties made me sad; some of the involvement ethos went and I decided it was time for me to go.

Others take a more philosophic view:

> I was deeply disappointed when PPA became The Pre-school Learning Alliance (PLA). I felt there was a change in emphasis, but perhaps now I recognise that society had begun to change and PPA had to change as well.

> PPA moved into being PLA and it wasn't just the name that changed. But even at the time, I recognised that this was what had to happen.

Some actively welcomed the new challenges it could bring:

> There were other views and ways of regarding parental responsibility and involvement. Playgroups were great places but not a lot of use for working mums.

> After three years on the National Executive Committee, I was ready for paid employment, but deeply attached to the work of PLA and exciting initiatives.

Moving on

Turning to the key issue of moving on viewed in retrospect, few mothers refer to the policy as such. Those who do (10) see the principle as an important part of the ethos:

> I was comfortable with the constitutional aspects – able to move on and went on to further my own career through a Postgraduate Certificate in Education.

> The moving on ethos made us look over our shoulders to grow a successor.

> We knew time was limited and went on to something more challenging – it kept us moving on to new things.

> It is imperative that people move on and others grow into the roles. I did not feel cut off, though some might.

> I am committed to moving on because it allows and encourages younger members to take your place and then grow themselves. Nobody is indispensable.

> In spite of a basic education, I was encouraged to take on roles and felt successful, therefore moving on was a natural progression.

> PPA helped me move on the whole time from the moment I was first asked to help run a playgroup, and was terrified, to being asked to take over a failing

primary school of over 400 pupils and accepting without reservation. Without PPA's support I might never have achieved so much.

It was a movement, so we expected to move on.

Nevertheless, it is clear that some moved on reluctantly:

To hang on bucks the development opportunities of others. Some are generous and share – others are not. It's the Queen Bee versus the Mother Hen.

The process, particularly in later years, was not always easy for practical reasons:

Moving on was difficult. Volunteers were less available. I felt trapped – not wanting to abandon ship, but feeling I had been around too long.

And there are some very sad memories:

Moving on was often too abrupt and forgetting.

It was difficult – not a happy time – it had to come.

Outcomes
Moving on – to what?
Whilst few mothers comment directly on 'moving on' as a policy, there are robust indications of its effects on what they went on to do. The overwhelming majority (85) consider that PPA really made a difference in their lives, and attest to benefiting from the opportunities offered to grow through the movement.

Skills
Firstly, they acquired skills that helped them in later life. Many, answering the question about acquisition of new skills, add comments such as 'undoubtedly', 'most certainly', 'a tremendous learning curve' and, 'may have had the skills before but PPA enabled me to strengthen them and to learn more'.

Skills, ranked in order of the number of people who said they had 'stood them in good stead over the years', are set out overleaf.

All 85 mothers mention communication and counselling skills. People management and committee work come second and third, followed closely by negotiating and coping with young children. Fundraising and how to cope with emergencies rank sixth and seventh but still with over half the mothers saying they learned how to cope with emergencies.

Skills ranked in order of importance	Number of respondents benefiting
Communication/counselling skills	85/100 mothers
People management	80
Committee work	79
Negotiating	76
Coping well with small children	73
Fundraising	65
How to cope with emergencies	56
Something else	28 (additional skills)

Additional skills range from how to make cooked playdough to speaking off the cuff and speaking in public; from anger management to bulk buying and from time management and conference organising to how to enjoy children.

How skills were used

The accounts of what happened next yield five clear themes:

1. 'PPA changed my life.'

These are words written by 26 mothers who feel the contrast between their lives before and during or after PPA very strongly. They express feelings of growing confidence, sometimes amounting to exhilaration, of finding a sense of purpose and fulfilment in their lives. Some had been excessively timid:

> a very lonely, shy mum, who knew nothing about young children and felt totally incompetent ... went back into teaching simply because PPA gave me the confidence to do it.

A few, suffering from depression or bereavement, had found the companionship of adults and being with children a turning point and a source of lasting strength:

> PPA was my lifeline.

Many more resemble the mother who says that she had hated her traditional grammar school and left it with one O level, knowing she was intelligent but deeply frustrated by the learning style. She played truant quite a lot:

> PPA turned my life around in terms of education and learning. PPA changed my life and helped me to discover the person I truly had the capacity to become.

She went on to gain a BA Honours in Sociology and Education and spent most of her working life developing play opportunities for children and young people.

2. 'PPA changed what I intended to do: I found my vocation.'
Twenty other mothers describe how their experiences in PPA resulted in them redirecting their careers and finding their vocation:

> Going back (to teaching in VI Form College) would have felt like going backwards. I had discovered all sorts of things I could do that I had not realised I was any good at. It made me a lot happier and was beneficial for all of us.

Some had trained to teach specialist subjects at secondary school level, or trained as nurses, or had worked in business or the public sector, but made their later careers in playgroups or as training and development officers or national advisers in the association, or became primary school teachers or worked in other early years professions and the health service:

> As an administrator in a large hospital, all PPA training came into play – having everything tried and tested.

Then there were those who used PPA skills through writing; others used them amongst families with complex needs, or through bereavement counselling or by offering support to those with Alzheimer's or in the hospice movement. A high proportion found their vocation in adult and second chance learning. They went on to teach in colleges of further education or in other institutions or to work in the voluntary sector:

> My involvement allowed me to grow, learn and develop and instilled attitudes and values that I have retained. I worked in Home-Start for 22 years.

Others, yet again, used their newfound skills in local authorities as under-fives advisers or in Ofsted. Through PPA, they

> ... had the confidence, the knowledge regarding childcare issues and increased ability to think through and find solutions.

A few went on to higher degrees. They contributed to early years knowledge and practice through university teaching and research.

3. 'Did I do this? What, me?'
However, for the largest sub-group of mothers (39 of 85) reflecting on the PPA experience and what it has meant for them in later life, the story is of raised aspirations and achievement, often recognised only in retrospect:

> How many mothers grew like me through the playgroup movement? How many said to themselves, as I did, 'No, I can't do it' – and yet still went ahead, and found the courage to do it?

This mother went on to tutor and to take the City and Guilds Teaching Certificate – 'What, me, who hated school?' Another said she was very shy and lacked confidence. She typifies the parent who went on to do things she had never even considered:

> I am what I am and I do what I do as a direct result of PPA. I became a much better nursery and infant teacher, with parental involvement on the agenda.

4. 'Paid and voluntary work go side by side.'

It is impossible to do justice to the variety of voluntary effort made by playgroup people later in life, usually in addition to paid employment, often in very demanding posts in the caring professions. Whilst some say they would probably have done it anyway, most connect their experience in the playgroup movement to equipping them with useful skills, and the motivation and the confidence to use them, together with the desire to give something back to the community:

> Practical skills learnt through the playgroup movement are of huge value for a bereavement volunteer who visits bereaved children and young people.

In addition to social care and teaching, PPA people have moved on to paid and unpaid work, becoming anything from elected parish, district and county councillors to churchwardens, from magistrates to family centre workers, from the National Trust to the Leonard Cheshire Foundation.[4]

5. An 'extra bonus?'

Mothers who are now grandmothers speak not only of the benefits of PPA for their own children (whilst also admitting some mistakes) but of the difference it has made to them in enjoying, understanding and relating to their grandchildren:

> Playgroup helped me understand and develop skills in my children and now helps me play with my grandchildren.

Another grandmother felt enabled to deal with the behaviour problems of a grandson with Asperger's syndrome. It can rub off on others too:

> My son says that he has learned from watching me with his son (10 months).

And again:

> Both girls were brought up on PPA – they were good on the phone when young and are both now working in education and involved in voluntary work.

Many others also write of the ways their children and grandchildren seem to have absorbed the self-help, community and child-focused character of PPA and to have been influenced by it in bringing up their own children and in their choice of career.

The number of mothers (39 out of 85) who said they had hated school themselves, yet went on to be school governors or active in parent-teacher associations suggests that PPA influenced at least some parents, who would not otherwise have done so, to actively participate in their children's later education. As one respondent who returned to secondary teaching commented:

> It was noticeable that mothers who helped in playgroup were the ones who went on to help in school, and to be members of the parent-teacher association (PTA).

Eighty five of the 100 respondents said that they had pursued careers and/or were active volunteers in various fields. The numbers involved in different occupations and activities are set out below.

Paid work

Occupation or activity	Number
Teaching, FE tutoring and lecturing in further education colleges and universities	68
Social work, child care advisers, OFSTED	20
Politics, set up own business, writers	9

Voluntary work and education

Parent-teacher associations, school governors	60
Went on to higher qualifications, degrees	20
The bench, politics	7

Paid and voluntary work, including service as trustees

VSO, CVO, CAB, Relate, Cruse, Samaritans, Volunteer Bureaux, Cancer Care, National Trust, Shelter, Housing, Age Concern etc.	44
Health – hospital administration, hospital governors, hospice, special needs, NAWCH, Alzheimer's	41
Scouts, Guides, parish councils, church work, etc.	36
Home-Start (co-ordinators/trustees); NCMA staff	16
Stayed in playgroup, became childminders, or specialised in play	16

Voluntary Service Overseas (VSO), Council for Voluntary Organisations (CVO), Citizens' Advice Bureau (CAB), National Association for the Welfare of Children in Hospital (NAWCH), National Childminding Association (NCMA)

Putting it into context – different worlds?

The three decades covered by this enquiry saw changes that those who started family life in the late 50s and 60s never envisaged. A mere twenty years after World War One devastated the lives of many of their parents, they lived as children and teenagers through the austerity and traumas of the 1939-45 war. It brought separation from parents through evacuation, temporary and sometimes permanent loss of fathers on active service, mothers working in factories, on the land or in hospitals in support of the war effort, fear of enemy attack and, for some, the Blitz. At the same time, they grew up in a culture of do it yourself and make do and mend. They enjoyed greater freedom to explore the world about them than young children do today and many benefited from changes following the 1944 Education Act.

After the war, women were again consigned to homemaking and to producing and rearing children. One mother's memories remind us of how it was for families in her village on the edge of town in the gestation period of playgroups:

> Young marrieds were moving in. Transport was by bus or your own feet ... It was pre the pill, when contraception was not considered an acceptable topic of conversation and when husbands came home for lunch on their bikes. There were no credit cards, few fridges or washing machines, the shops were a three-mile walk there and back ... no double-glazing and no central heating ...

> The larger issues for us to worry about ... were the neutron bomb and the Cold War – we were so afraid for our children. Childcare advice was the health visitor or the family ... However, everyone wanted the best for their kids and a channel for their frustrated skills.

Consider the speed of ensuing political, economic and social changes discussed in other chapters and it can come as no surprise that the playgroup movement changed in the wake of new knowledge and changing economic and social needs – particularly those of working mothers. It changed in the course of the three decades under review: rapidly, from campaigning for nursery schools to self-help playgroups for families and communities; more slowly but inexorably to becoming a service. Nor is it surprising that those volunteers who experienced the urgency, the excitement, the freedom to learn and the satisfaction of creating or participating in a life-affirming experience unimpeded by lots of rules should feel the loss of something that was, for children and their mothers, at the heart of the early playgroup movement: freedom to play.

Concluding comments
A particular experience of play
Freedom to play and freedom to learn emerge as the two characteristics of the early playgroup movement that have been increasingly eroded by changing needs, mores and legislation.

A theory of children's play as an art form, developed by Peter Slade (1954,1958) in relation to child drama, maintains that the only true distinction that develops in play is between projected and personal play.

Projected play is usually quiet and absorbing. It is play in which objects of interest and affection outside oneself are the focus of attention. In young children, it may be dolls, bricks, a rattle, even kindling or cardboard boxes. This type of play develops observation, patience and organisation. In personal play, in contrast, the whole person or self is used: 'I am the king', '...cook', '...doctor' or '...nurse'. Slade held (1954) that, 'man is happy or unhappy in so far as he discovers the right admixture of these quite distinct manners of using energy. Lack of play may mean a permanent lost part of oneself' (*ibid*).

Creating freedom for both children and mothers in playgroups to play together, exploring through all the senses, meant (*ibid*, 1958) that children were, ' discovering life and self through emotional and physical attempt, and then through physical practice (dramatic play in which all are doers)'. In addition, mothers had a second chance not only for projected play (with words, figures and ideas), but also for personal play in which they could be the speaker, the organiser, the initiator in the safety of the facilitating environment.

Such opportunities, whereby some mothers found their vocations and others who had not enjoyed school found pleasure in learning and went on to fulfilling careers, have been largely lost in the swing to providing professional services to meet the needs of today's working parents.

Nevertheless, current economic circumstances coupled with the growth of organisations such as Women Like Us[3] that connect women and flexible work, and those that are committed to 'establishing new structures that provide capabilities for people ... to participate meaningfully and creatively in the life of society in less materialistic ways' (Jackson, 2009:11) may lead again to opportunities for parents who choose to do so to spend more time with their young children and to reap the benefits.[4]

Was PPA unique?

Clearly, 'unique' – defined in the OED as 'unmatched, unequalled, having no like, or equal or parallel' – is not applicable to many of the attributes most valued by respondents: lasting friendships, confidence building, a lifeline, life-long learning, being involved and responsible for undertakings and projects felt to be supremely worthwhile, all of which have been recorded in relation to other organisations and activities. Such experiences can be and are, of course, unique for an individual.

In chapter 2 it is suggested and persuasively argued that PPA's uniqueness lies in the creation of a facilitating environment in which mothers and children could all develop in ways appropriate for that stage in life, that were beneficial for both. Analysis of responses to this enquiry suggests an additional benefit of such a facilitating environment and, if Peter Slade's theories are correct, an explanation of why so many mothers, especially the most diffident and reluctant, grew in the ways they did.

A quiet revolution

The playgroup movement did not set out to be a feminist movement and yet, without aggressiveness, it made a tremendous difference to the lives and the choices available to thousands of women. A recurring theme comes from mothers who recognised the part played by PPA in that wider freedom:

> In the seventies and eighties women were still regarded as second-class citizens. I think women today do not realise what we achieved for them. We

were the quiet revolution, beavering away to remove some of the prejudices that were around.

PPA changed my political and social outlook. It was my introduction to feminism in a safe, supportive environment.

PPA was never seen as a women's organisation – but when you think about the way it has influenced and changed some women's lives ... Wow!

Qualities that count

But what conclusions can we realistically draw from this enquiry? It rests on the recollections of a small proportion of the mothers involved in early play-groups. Fifty years on, incomplete and subjective, these can only partially illuminate any longer-term consequences of the policy for some of those who actually 'moved on'. Because everybody could 'move on' does not mean that everybody did so, nor 'that moving' on was a positive experience for everyone.

Nevertheless, responses provide clear evidence of the power of the 'moving on' policy to extend learning opportunities. It did enable mothers in successive generations to enjoy their children and understand children's needs, to develop existing skills that contributed positively to their family lives, their future careers and those of their children and possibly their grandchildren.

Findings also demonstrate that the process of moving on through a variety of pathways engaged, motivated and enabled many mothers who had left school without qualifications or ambitions to widen their horizons. These mothers developed a 'lust for learning' through PPA experience and courses. They achieved far more than they had ever thought possible, especially in the fields of social services, early years and adult education, and the voluntary sector. The number of 'just mums' who grew as parents was reflected in the exceptional demand for PPA courses and the observations of tutors in further education colleges (Shinman, 1986).

Almost every return in this enquiry, through recurring words and phrases, holds clues to what helped make it happen. The vital conditions for this level of personal growth and development are:

Being able to make mistakes without losing face

Everyone recognised as having something of value to offer

Learning by observation and recollection

Respect (for children and adults)

Non-judgemental listening

A 'together we can do it' approach – community action

No passing or failing

Doing, not talking and being told

Having fun

Hard work

Trust

Feeling happy

Taking responsibility.

This ethos, perhaps driven by the coming together of perceived needs of children and of opportunities for mothers, reached and included many who had not benefited from opportunities offered at school. It was an ethos rooted in the nature and quality of relationships, and was the antithesis of a deficit model of parenting.

In contrast, today's increased insistence on telling, measuring, testing (failing) and qualifications – valuable though they may be – could, for important minorities, have unintended consequences. They can prevent parents achieving their potential. There is still a great deal to learn, or relearn, about making social inclusion a reality and retaining important principles.

These principles, including the open-ended opportunities for personal growth that were both offered and motivated by an organisation such as PPA once was, could profitably be reinstated in our current society, in which we are going to have to look hard at ways to harness people's skills and learning potential in a harsh economic climate.

Notes

1 Area organisers first emerged informally and were later appointed by branches in consultation with other levels of PPA. AOs visited and supported the playgroups and mother and toddler groups in the area covered by their branch, linking the groups to the PPA network. They also liaised with statutory and other voluntary bodies. Most were paid their out-of-pocket expenses and some received token payment.

2 A complete list of organisations and bodies in which respondents went on to work in a paid or voluntary capacity gives an idea of the spread of PPA's influence and can be found on the PPA website (playgroupmovement.org.uk).

3 More information from www.womenlikeus.org.uk

4 See also *Backing the Future* from www.neweconomics.org and www.actionforchildren.org .

6

The failure of PPA to define its ideology

Charlotte Williamson

Without intellectual and theoretical underpinnings, no movement can succeed. (Carolyn Heilbrun, feminist literary scholar, 1989)

I think we never fully understood ourselves. (Helen Smith, long-standing PPA member, 2009, personal communication)

The Pre-school Playgroups Association (PPA) was a new social movement. It was also a new organisation of extraordinary promise and, for some years, of extraordinary success. But PPA failed to secure for young children and their parents the sort of provision for play – parent-run playgroups – that it believed could best support the emotional, intellectual and social growth of both mothers and children. The reasons for this failure are complex, but one major factor contributed to it: PPA's lack of an explicit ideology.

Although PPA never had an explicit ideology, by the early 1970s PPA members had intuitively arrived at a set of ideas that captured their beliefs about what they were doing. They used words in ways that both reflected and created those beliefs: words such as 'play', 'community playgroups' and '(personal) growth'. Members had also developed a set of principles, rules for action, that both guided and reflected their implicit ideology. The principles included:

1. *The value of play in itself, not just of learning through play.*

2. *Respect for children and childhood,* including respect for the parent-child bond and respect for the child's parents. (PPA did not adopt a deficit model of parents as needing to be improved, though it knew that parents, like everyone, may need help occasionally.)

3. *Parents' responsibility for, and essential part in, their children's learning.* This was a major point of conflict with the state's services.

4. *'Moving on'.* This ensured that only parents whose children were in the playgroup ran it and took part in the rota of mother-helpers. It kept parents and children together in the playgroup; met parents' passionate wish to provide the best for their own and other children; and gave new playgroup parents the opportunities for the learning and the satisfaction that earlier playgroup parents had had.

5. *Valuing everyone* for their contributions to the playgroup and to all the activities connected with the playgroup – committee, fundraising, work for the wider community. Parents are rewarded by their children's love but can also find inspiration, a quickening of the imagination, through adults' appreciation.

6. *Enabling parents to experience new challenges* and develop new skills, and take on new roles. This mirrored what parents do in introducing their children to the outside world, encouraging and approving their exploration of it.

7. *Courses that did not give qualifications.* Courses were about how to manage play and playgroups in order to give children the best experiences possible. They built on course members' experiences and views of what they needed to learn about. Courses were not about judging members' abilities or progress. They did not mimic professional training with its rigidities and qualifications.

These principles captured the essence of PPA's ideas and feelings. But PPA members did not draw from these principles the implicit ideology that underlay them. PPA thus lacked an explicit ideology to guide its members' actions and explain them to the outside world, a set of ideas in tune with its members' feelings and intuitions, a set of ideas that could be supported by theoretical justifications. Ten years after its beginning, the movement had not reached that stage in its intellectual and political development. Before it reached that stage, it was overtaken by events that changed it forever.

Three consequences followed from this lack of an explicit ideology:

1. Because PPA did not articulate its ideology clearly, it did not always act in accordance with it nor transmit it to each new generation of its members, the playgroup parents and the local and national volunteers.

2. In particular, ideas from outside that might conflict with PPA's implicit ideology were not always recognised as being in conflict. When in 1973 an organisational structure that did not support PPA's implicit ideology was recommended by an outside body, PPA adopted it uncritically.

3. Successful social movements do make a difference; that is the point of them. But without a strong and clear ideology to present to the outside world, PPA could not get its message to that world and whatever difference that message might have made was lost. Instead, PPA succumbed to pressures from outside itself: pressures from the government, from wider social changes and from expectations that put a low value on women not in paid employment and a high value on paid, and especially on professional, work.

This chapter is about the first two of these consequences. Chapter 7 is mainly about the third.

PPA as a social movement

Social movements arise in response to some aspect of life that begins to seem wrong or deficient to one or a few people who believe that others will join with them in working for change (Mansbridge and Morris, 2001; Rowbotham, 2004). They commonly form a group of like-minded people and begin to take action together, social action. So it was with playgroups and with the organisation that was formed to support and promote playgroups: PPA. (See chapter 1.)

Taking social action can create new meanings as well as new structures. After mothers had started and run playgroups as temporary substitutes for nursery schools, they began to experience benefits to themselves as well as to their children. What had started as a pragmatic response to a lack of nursery schools became the discovery of a more creative and more rewarding way of doing things. Thus many parents came to think that parent-run playgroups were better for their children and for themselves than nursery schools. Their belief that they should be responsible for and take part in their children's pre-school learning was contrary to nursery schools' practice and philosophy.

These beliefs were radical: they went against the status quo, society's acceptance of the value of professionally run and staffed nursery schools. As in other social movements, there were potential tensions between this radical position and conservative positions. PPA members who ran playgroups without a management or governance committee of parents, or without mothers voluntarily staffing the playgroup on a rota alongside the supervisor, or who continued to believe that nursery schools were desirable for all children, took conservative positions. These different convictions and the tensions they created were there from the beginning of the movement and continued, as can be seen in letters in *Contact*. In 1982, for example, a mother who ran a playgroup sent her own children to nursery school because she found a mothers' rota tiresome and because local nursery schools did not allow mothers to stay (Turner, 1982).

Nevertheless, difficulties and tensions were kept at bay during the early years of the movement by the exhilaration and momentum created by a large number of positive factors: the rapid increase in the numbers of playgroups; the excellence of local and national PPA publications; the help unstintingly given to playgroups by other playgroups, by voluntary local fieldworkers (called area organisers) and branches, and, later, by county associations and regional committees; the excitement, pleasure and rewards felt by many parents at all levels of the movement; and a growing official recognition of the value of playgroups.

Indeed, some tensions probably benefit from not being articulated in the very early stages of a new social movement. Members need time and experience to compare practices and ideas amongst themselves; to identify what values and principles they hold in common and why; to look at related social movements; to analyse their position in relation to the rest of society; and to decide on their major objectives. Sometimes those objectives may be different from the ones they started with, sometimes so different that the new objectives could not have been foreseen by the members or by anyone else at the earliest stages of the movement (Toch, 1965). Members' actions, the meanings they give them and the new knowledge that action and meaning create can 'open the door to vistas that had seemed too glaring before' (Toch, 1965:238).

This time of gestation, of the creation of something that did not exist before, may extend over several generations of members, with intermittent conflicts over principles, values and objectives. Conflicts of convictions may lead to schisms when some members split away from the main movement. Or members and their opposing convictions may remain within a movement, competing to be recognised as its authentic voice. But eventually, a social movement must formulate its unique ideology, put into words the ideas that guide its members' actions and explain them to the outside world. It must show that it is different from other movements or organisations like it: it must separate itself pragmatically and ideologically from them. Then it has a chance of surviving as a social movement.

By the late 1960s and early 1970s, PPA members had intuitively, with very little theory beyond that about the value of play to young children, created 'an institutional framework that will maximise [its members'] own growth,' as well as that of members' children (Sutherland, 1973:22). By 'institutional framework', Dr Sutherland meant the parent-run playgroups, the local and national arrangements for their promotion and support, and the relationships that held them all together. At every level, PPA intuitively fostered the conditions that social scientists deem rewarding: demanding and varied tasks; work that needs and gives opportunities for learning; decision-making; relevance to life; optimism and a feeling that the future is important; and ready opportunities to advance to greater responsibility and leadership because these opportunities are not blocked (Emery and Thorsrud, 1959; Sofer, 1961). Creating and maintaining an organisation that fosters the emotional, intellectual and social growth of its members and their capacity for creative relationships is uncommon. It is also difficult (Obholzer and Roberts, 1994). Yet the course for PPA, with its parent-run playgroups, the richness of its volunteering and the enthusiasm and joyfulness of many of its members, seemed set fair. Many PPA members probably understood the implicit ideology that lay under their actions, but they understood it in an almost mystical sense and were not quite ready to put it into clear and explicit words. That left PPA vulnerable to confusion and misunderstanding, both outside the movement and within it. Moreover, all was not well with PPA's governance body at national level, the National Executive Committee (NEC).

PPA as an organisation at national level

By the late 1960s, PPA had a national governance body, the National Executive Committee, the successor to the original group of people who got together after Belle Tutaev's letter. The NEC saw itself as responding to the needs of playgroups, not as directing playgroups' actions. It copied the committee structure of parent-run playgroups. It was made up of 17-19 voluntary (unpaid) members invited, elected or co-opted from local PPA groups, branches or (later) regional associations. It appointed one, later two, national advisers, analogous to supervisors in playgroups. Like supervisors, advisers were paid staff, who could remain in post as long as their work satisfied their employers. Like supervisors, the advisers attended all committee meetings and could exert a good deal of influence by giving or withholding advice. To cover administrative matters, the NEC created the post of general secretary. The first person to hold this post was a former chair of the NEC.

All the NEC members and its staff shared a commitment to a common purpose and to each other, all giving of their best. Their shared values and shared work gave members a sense of achievement and joy, like that of playgroup parents. As well as making crucial decisions, and exercising responsibility and leadership, NEC members had to learn new skills and develop expertise in new fields such as editing publications, handling publicity and applying for funds. In these ways, the NEC and parent-run playgroups mirrored each other. But by the early 1970s, NEC members had begun to experience intolerable workloads. Some remedy was needed.

A voluntary organisation growing in size and in success has choices about how to manage heavy demands upon its national executive or governance committee members. It can disband. It can carry on but limit its scope. It can appoint paid staff.

Appointing administrative staff can benefit a voluntary organisation. Secretarial support for active voluntary members in key roles, and imaginative help such as loans of office equipment, the short-term appointment of research assistants for particular projects, honoraria or allowances so that speakers can appear on platforms without ladders in their tights, can also be provided to ease members' work. Appointing professional staff, by contrast, can cause problems if they have the same sorts of knowledge and skills and undertake the same sorts of work as the key volunteers. Whether professional staff should be appointed needs careful consideration because such appointments can impair the value of the organisation for its key voluntary members and can change the organisation's nature.

What choices an organisation makes depends on its purposes and the sources of its funding. PPA already had funding from the Department of Education and Science for its two national advisers, appointed in 1967 and 1971, and in 1972 applied to the Department of Health and Social Security for funding for eight field staff, who were called training and development officers. This was a usual way for the UK government to help voluntary organisations. It gave the government some control over the voluntary organisation by pushing it towards appointing paid staff rather than supporting volunteers. Members were desperate for help and appointed their first field staff (TDOs) in 1972. But the NEC gave them no instructions about what to do (chapter 7). Given time, a new kind of volunteer-staff relationship could perhaps have been worked out by drawing on the NEC members' and the TDOs' intuitions of what each felt to be right. But in 1973, the NEC was offered free consultation and advice from the international consultants, McKinsey and Co. Unfortunately, McKinsey's advice was given and accepted before PPA had had enough experience and time to work out new relationships congruent with its implicit ideology. McKinsey's advice ran contrary to PPA's ideology; but members did not see this in time to reject that advice.

The inability of PAA to make its ideology explicit

Some social scientists, politicians and commentators in the early 1970s re-cognised and praised PPA's success in creating through the intuitions of its members institutional structures that could maximise their own and their young children's growth. But one well-wisher, Kay Carmichael, the distin-guished Scottish social work academic (1925-2009), warned PPA in April 1973 that intuition on its own was not enough: it had to be joined by thought (Car-michael, 1973).

That warning was timely. NEC members and other members at national level thought well pragmatically, when working on publications, the constitution and so on. But they did not think well analytically. 'We were not [analytic] thinkers' (national member, speaking in 2009 of the early 1970s). Members did not stand back and examine the springs of their actions, their deepest feelings, fears and hopes. Some staff and some members seemed to have almost an aversion to analytic thought, seeing it as harmful to the beliefs and purposes of PPA. How this aversion came about in a group of people charged with the leadership of ideas and strategic thought in a young and growing organisation is hard to understand. Many factors played a part. Some were the consequences of beliefs good in themselves but politically inept. In that lay the tragic paradox of PPA.

1. Many PPA members were empirically rather than theoretically minded. In the early 1970s, they were still exploring their own actions, still creating the meanings of their playgroup work and of their extended work at local or national levels. 'We didn't know what we were doing until we had done it' (Sheila Shinman, personal communication, 2010). 'We never really arrived at a consistent, confident belief in our uniqueness and rightness' (Helen Smith, personal communication, 2010).

2. The essence of the experiences, feelings and ideas that motivated mem-bers, the ways in which their love for their own children, rewarded by their children's love for them, found expression through work for other children, for other families and for the wider community, was hard to put into words. It still is.

3. Most NEC members and their national advisers valued feelings and intui-tions highly and feared that analytic thought could spoil warmth and good relationships. The view that feeling and thought were antithetical was dan-gerous because the reverse is more likely to be true. 'I feel strongly and I think strongly: but I seldom feel without thinking or think without feeling,' said Coleridge (1796). NEC members seem not to have understood that intuition,

the immediate apperception of an idea or situation without conscious reasoned thought, and often accompanied by a rush of feeling, does not depend solely on sensitivity and sensibility. It depends also on knowledge and experience. Many NEC members and staff were familiar with nursery education and with the theories of mother-child relationships and of play current amongst educated people in the 1960s. But NEC members failed to realise that this taken-for-granted knowledge was partly the basis of the intuitions they prized so highly.

Analytic thought breaks down assumptions, separates out differences, identifies likenesses and rearranges old ideas in order to build up new ones. So it is potentially constructive. But radical thoughts can feel destructive to those who have them and thus engender guilt and a wish to return to the *status quo*, to conservatism and safety.

4. Members did not want to hurt or exclude mothers or children in any form of pre-school provision. PPA should be broad church, open door, inclusive, welcoming all mothers and young children. Members saw mothers of young children as vulnerable; no disapproval of their choices and actions should be voiced. Nursery schools, playgroups run for profit or without a committee of parents, playgroups that provided poor play material or ill-judged interventions with children, that had low standards of play, must be accepted into PPA membership. To declare openly that, ideally, parent-run playgroups were better for parents and children than even good nursery schools was emotionally and intellectually difficult. In any case, it was necessary to acquire as many members as possible, both to finance the organisation and to give it credibility. Expediency and principle reinforced each other.

5. Many PPA members wished for unity within the movement and for cordial relations with those outside it. The wish for unity probably led to the fear that open conflict over ideas might damage the movement. The causes of disunity, such as members' radical or conservative convictions, were not identified and scrutinised. Similarly, attempts were made to establish good relations with organisations such as the National Union of Teachers, who openly expressed hostility towards playgroups and PPA (Paterson, 1974). To uphold the value of ordinary parents' knowledge and intuitions against the expertise of educational, social work and health professionals was difficult and required far more scientific evidence and argument than PPA could muster.

6. Some key members had backgrounds in education. Though highly relevant to PPA's work in most ways, educationalists tend to take a deficit view of

parents. Traces of this attitude were unhelpful in an organisation that wanted to value 'ordinary' parents.

7. NEC members and the newly appointed TDOs were often too busy, too pressed for time and energy, to think analytically about policy or to read theoretical or academic works. They took radical action without stopping to recognise that their actions were radical or why they were. So they lacked theoretical justification for their ideas and actions. In this, they were like some other radical groups and social movements that started in the early 1960s, for example, the patient movement (Williamson, 2010).

These aspects of national PPA in the early 1970s were barriers to the analytic thought necessary to articulate an explicit ideology. Lack of a clear, explicit and coherent ideology that expressed what members felt intuitively, and lack of theoretical and intellectual underpinnings to it, were dangerous, if they prevented PPA members from being able to assess what was and what was not in the long term interests of children, parents and the social movement. They were especially dangerous if attack should come from outside before PPA was ready for it or did not recognise it as an attack. Attack did come, in the guise of McKinsey's advice to the NEC.

McKinsey and Company

When the NEC in 1973 accepted the free consultation from McKinsey and Co, members believed they would be offered an organisational structure tailored to the specific needs of their own unique organisation. Instead McKinsey re-commended clarifying an hierarchical structure for staff and increasing their number (McKinsey and Co, 1973). That advice was broadly the standard voluntary organisation model: a few paid administrative and field (profes-sional) staff and many volunteers, from whom NEC members would con-tinue to be elected. More staff would carry more of the day-to-day workload. They were to have a separate system of accountability. Professionalism was to be fostered in them (McKinsey and Co, 1973). The NEC members were to be the organisation's policy makers; the staff were to carry out those policies.

What that model overlooks is that knowledge, and hence authority derived from that knowledge (sapiential authority) come from doing day-to-day tasks at every level of complexity and importance. Removing these tasks from policy makers prevents them from knowing as much as their paid profes-sional staff. It leaves them dependent on staff's advice rather than on their own collective knowledge and judgement. We can see this in many voluntary and statutory organisations. But it was a particularly inappropriate model for PPA for additional reasons.

1. The NEC voluntary members symbolised ordinary parents in playgroups. NEC members also represented – in the sense that they spoke for and were elected by – the 'ordinary' parent members countrywide. It was impossible to separate completely the tasks of voluntary members from those of paid staff at any level of the organisation, from playgroup to NEC. Nor was it desirable, for in the long run separation removes from volunteers the opportunities for experiencing the challenges and rewards of certain tasks. That threatens the volunteers' opportunities for learning, for personal development and for exercising the leadership of ideas.

2. Regarding TDOs as professionals with salaries gave them rewards beyond the salary itself. Staff's expenses were paid at a higher rate than those of NEC members or of voluntary fieldworkers. Staff had personal secretaries; volunteers a small typing allowance. Staff held regular development sessions and away days with the national advisers; NEC members and other key volunteers at national level had no training for specific roles and no regular meetings for mutual support and in-depth discussions. Staff could afford to attend advanced training days put on by other organisations because their grants from the DHSS had a training component; volunteers could not afford this training. These extra practical benefits to staff privileged them over the volunteers. It reinforced the higher value McKinsey's recommendations put on them than on volunteers and on 'ordinary' parents.

3. Introducing professionals into PPA went against a view held by many people in the 1960s and 1970s, including the psychoanalyst D W Winnicott, that professionals' actions and advice could harm babies and young children (Winnicott, 1957). So the term's connotations were unfortunate. It implied, too, that volunteers could not act professionally in the sense of acting with skill and dedication.

4. Staff, including the national advisers, had security of tenure; volunteers were transient, moving on. Staff could acquire knowledge, build up expertise, establish long-term working relationships with staff of other local or national organisations, statutory and voluntary, in ways voluntary members could not. The discrepancy between the tenure of staff and members of governance bodies is a problem for democratic societies (Dahrendorf, 1974). Civil servants, his example, can gain 'illegitimate, though often involuntary' power over elected members of Parliament (Dahrendorf, 1974:693). His solution was to limit officials' terms of office.

5. The consequences for the TDOs, the new professional field staff, were not entirely happy, either. A new hierarchy of accountability put them under the

national advisers' care and authority. It deprived them of some of the freedoms of expression and action that NEC members took for granted for themselves and that are the essence of the voluntary principle. Some TDOs felt they had lost the freedom to speak as they chose. They had to ask advice for all but routine activities and keep diaries of time spent. They felt that NEC members regarded them as second-class citizens and wanted to put them into leading reins (Henderson, 1978). One or two TDOs who had been NEC members complained about these restrictions. Unfortunately this was interpreted as their personal difficulties in adjusting to their new role rather than as a warning about the role itself.

6. NEC members' rewards were intangible and they remained accountable to each other and to the members who elected them. Having two structures of reward and accountability in any organisation tends to weaken the motivation of the members of each (Etzioni, 1961). Voluntary workers, envying paid workers' salaries, can think, 'Why should I do all this work for nothing?' Paid workers, envying voluntary workers' freedom, can think, 'Why should I work beyond my contract?' These feelings tend to neutralise and demotivate each other unless one gains influence or power over the other (Etzioni, 1961). Here, the scene was set for the tenured field staff to gain power over the transient voluntary office-holders at national, regional and local levels.

These changes to organisational structure were contrary to PPA's implicit ideological belief that parents working voluntarily, from love for their own and other children, were uniquely valuable. Not just a necessary workforce, they were people whose playgroup and wider PPA experiences could enrich their own lives and that of the community round them. But the changes potentially worked against active members' opportunities and abilities to contribute to the thought and work of the organisation as fully as they might wish, unless they sought and gained staff posts. (That was a possible move for some volunteers but one others did not want.) Moreover, splitting the TDOs from the volunteers carrying out the same tasks with equal commitment and competence potentially destroyed the sense of sharing and of equality that was a joyful aspect of PPA at every level. There were only a few TDOs and they were tactful, as chapter 7 describes. But PPA was no longer an organic whole; something had been lost. For PPA, this may have been the most serious consequence of all.

The stress that the McKinsey recommendations, once they began to be implemented, caused to PPA was at first located at national level, within the NEC and some TDOs. But the scene was set in 1973 for wider tensions and consequences, as chapter 7 describes.

Accepting McKinsey

Outlining the disadvantages of the McKinsey proposals more than thirty years after they were put forward raises the question, why did the NEC accept them? The simplest answer is that we did not fully understand that McKinsey was a management consultancy designed to help top executives in commercial companies improve the efficiency and profits of their companies. PPA was not such a company. Reciprocally, McKinsey did not fully understand us (Lee Fairlie, TDO, personal communication, 2010). McKinsey interviewed few members at national or at any level. In any case, with our lack of an explicit ideology and our unresolved tensions over radical and conservative positions amongst those who took part in NEC meetings (NEC members, the general secretary and the national advisers), we probably were difficult to understand, particularly by consultants with a commercial, executive perspective. They and we were at cross purposes as well as confused.

We certainly did not know that the consultant who advised us, Ed Berman, had an agenda of his own, to professionalise voluntary organisations (Berman, 2004). If we had understood that, it is unlikely that we would have accepted McKinsey. Professionalism can have harmful aspects and consequences; professionals in the human services tend to reduce the opportunities of clients to exercise responsibility and autonomy (Johnson, 1972). That did not fit with PPA's ideas about supporting parents' responsibility, authority and personal development. Some members of the NEC did feel disquiet. We did not express it firmly or clearly enough; and we were easily deflected by the pragmatic circumstance that the first TDOs were already in post by the time the disadvantages of the new structure began to become apparent. Feelings of goodwill towards the TDOs, allied to a fear of seeming unkind or harsh, a grave sin in PPA where good feeling was everything, inhibited action.

In 2009, I asked some PPA members who, like me, had been active at national level in the early 1970s why we had accepted the McKinsey recommendations. They answered, 'dazzled by experts,' 'advice free,' 'exciting to be advised by renowned management consultants,' 'pressure to accept in order to gain the grants from the DHSS,' 'recommendations congenial to key players.'

The other question – why did some members not oppose these proposals? – is less easy to answer. But the reasons overlap with those that inhibited national PPA from articulating a clear ideology. They included members' reliance on intuition without accompanying analytic thought. But whereas intuition had worked well in creating the new institutions of playgroups and the systems that supported them, it did not work well in helping NEC members oppose proposals that might harm those institutions. NEC members had not had enough experience in other organisations or know enough organisational theory to be able to identify the risks of the proposed structure or to draw from their own intuition ideas to argue rationally (or at all) against those proposals.

Most PPA members were women who had little experience of organisations. The NEC at that time had a chairman but its other members and its senior staff were women. In the early 1970s, some contemporary feminist writers considered that feminine thought and women's fear of taking power and of expressing anger kept women intellectually weak and politically naïve (Heilbrun, 1989). This can perhaps be put more positively as an aspect of women's ethical sense of connectedness to others, in contrast to men's more individualistic ethical sense (Gilligan, 1982). But political naïvety in a world of small-p and large-p politics does not serve organisations well. PPA's feminine culture of gentleness and of avoiding or damping down conflict was salient, too. PPA was an organisation in which people trusted that each other's intentions and actions were good.

Above all, the views of key people prevailed. The NEC chairman, and the NEC member who succeeded him as chair, strongly favoured McKinsey. Both had been local authority councillors. They were accustomed to the statutory organisations' model of powerful councillors (or members of parliament), acting in accordance with large-p political ideologies and policies, with the obedient help of large numbers of paid administrative and professional staff (or civil servants). That model's defect in allowing paid staff to gain greater effective power than the councillors (or MPs) had been clear to academics and political commentators for some time; but in the 1970s had not perhaps been fully unfolded to councillors themselves. For PPA, lacking an explicit ideology, the risks of dominance by staff were even greater. Then, too, the position of the general secretary and the national advisers was awkward, since they were paid, permanent staff. What they thought and how far they argued for their views outside NEC meetings is obscure. As far as I can remember at NEC meetings, two supported and one did not oppose the chairman's views.

The advantages of the McKinsey proposals

The McKinsey proposals had advantages. They created a cadre of highly committed and competent field staff who could take forward PPA's work in advising and encouraging playgroups, organising courses, speaking in public and so on, just as active volunteers were already doing. Indeed, the first TDOs appointed were all active PPA members. This benefited PPA by ensuring that the TDOs knew the movement well and felt in accord with it. It also showed again that the tensions arising from their appointments were structural, not personal; but we were too unsophisticated to realise that.

The tensions continue

Tensions between the voluntary and field staff members continued to arise. At the 1977 AGM, a motion that the tenure of TDOs be restricted – that the transience or moving on principle be applied to them – was put forward but defeated. In 1979 renewed tensions resulted in the setting up of a Staff Insight Group, described in chapter 7. Most of the group's members were field staff and it was chaired by a national adviser who had been particularly sympathetic to the TDOs in their early difficult days. The group sought to distinguish between the roles of key volunteers and field staff. The hope that redefining roles will relieve stress is common in organisations. But when people are doing the same things, whether from wish or necessity, simple separation is not possible. Here the group decided that staff must play a more central role in PPA, while empowering and supporting the volunteers (chapter 7).

The NEC accepted this way of looking at the organisation, thus legitimising the Staff Insight Group's decision. By then, with the TDOs long in post and working well, it would have been difficult for the NEC to do anything else, especially since the NEC members in the early 1980s were different from those of 1973. Turn-over of the elected members of governance bodies characterises democracies. But it can lose continuity of knowledge about an organisation's unwritten history, and important insights and reservations about policies may perish.

Once one group of people can legitimately see themselves as empowering and supporting members of another group, they have become dominant over it, whether they intended to or not. Once one group of people sees another group as in need of its special help, as clients, relationships can easily become asymmetrical. Equality and unity can die. The baby birds hatched out by the NEC's acceptance of the McKinsey proposals in 1973 had put on fine feathers by the 1980s and come home to roost.

McKinsey – the aftermath

What were the consequences for PPA of accepting the McKinsey proposals? Young social movements are vulnerable in their early stages: probably more fail than succeed. PPA showed that it is dangerous not to articulate an explicit, clear and courageous ideology as soon as it becomes possible. What is implicit must be made explicit. Without a clear ideology, members' decisions may inadvertently impair the movement's purposes.

Another factor that, together with the lack of a clear ideology, probably increased PPA's vulnerability was its policy of moving on. Moving on was intended to mirror the natural changes in parents' preoccupations, concerns and satisfactions as their children's development moves on from each stage to the next. It was also intended to ensure that the opportunities for growth, responsibility and leadership that each generation of playgroup parents had enjoyed was passed on to the next generation:

> Each new generation of parents must have opportunities to discover for themselves what a playgroup is about, and be convinced that they, themselves, need to play a part if the aims are to be realised' (Codling *et al*, 1978:25).

But without an explicit ideology, a framework to guide members' actions, moving on could leave playgroups vulnerable to ups and downs in playgroup parents' and supervisors' understanding, with the loss of those very opportunities for personal growth that were part of the objective of moving on.

In addition, lack of explicitness about why PPA ways of doing things were valuable could easily let playgroups lose the practical knowledge of playgroup people who knew about play, about the responsibilities and procedures of committees, and so on (Keeley, 1974). Established playgroups had some continuity or overlap of parents as children grew from 3 to 4, then left.

But these were short generation times and things could change quickly. In constantly re-creating the early days of playgroups with novice mothers learning what to do from scratch, PPA overlooked how each generation in any context normally builds on the work and discoveries of the generations that have gone before it. Each new person comes fresh to a particular experience; but the nature of the experience is usually influenced by their predecessors. A PPA publication said approvingly in 1975:

> Those who learn by doing tend to be reluctant to set down their learning on paper, since suggestions so easily become prescriptions. (PPA, 1975)

But prescriptions may be right; and if they are wrong or no longer fit new circumstances, they can be changed. Ideas about good playgroup practices and the reasons for them needed to be written down and handed on within each established playgroup, lest they be lost. Playgroups just starting needed a quick source of guidance and inspiration, just as new PPA members needed to know PPA's ideology.

Moving on also moved experienced PPA members out of the movement. Active volunteers could move on over the years from playgroup through branch, county and regional associations to national committees and the NEC. But ultimately they had to leave PPA unless they became paid staff. That lost dedicated champions of the voluntary principle, as well as losing experienced volunteers' knowledge and insights and leaving new volunteers weak in relation to the tenured staff. One of the goals that McKinsey proposed for PPA in 1973 was to 'encourage and promote the growth of individuals beyond the playgroup stage' (McKinsey and Co, 1973). That was a reasonable goal, although every stage of life has its own value and should be lived for its own sake. But it is an odd organisation that prepares its members for roles outside itself but does not devise some way of retaining their goodwill, experience, knowledge and capacity for thought, once they are no longer active in the day-to-day work.

Could PPA have acted differently?

In posing this question, we have to ask, 'What could we have known at the time?' Management consultants like McKinsey and Co were already suspect (Patrick Sills, lecturer in organisational analysis, personal communication, 1977). We knew about the Tavistock Institute of Human Relations but we did not seek its advice. The Tavistock might have used its empirical and theoretical knowledge about relationships in organisations, about the springs of creativity and about the dangers of thinking that tasks can be detached from feelings, to guide us towards an organisational structure that fitted our ideology. Alternatively, we might have been able to devise a structure ourselves, had analytic thought been valued instead of shunned.

Had we understood the risks of separating members into volunteers and paid professional staff, we could have asked the government or charities for money to fund, not a few paid field staff, but large numbers of active volunteers. Volunteers are by definition not paid; but they can be given generous expenses and benefits in kind: training occasions, meetings for mutual support, excellent clerical and administrative help – the kinds of benefits that were given to the TDOs. Parts of a network of volunteers were already in place, in voluntary area organisers and tutors who advised clusters of playgroups and arranged local courses. This network could have been extended into a comprehensive system of experienced volunteers, working for as few or as many hours as suited them. Generous expenses for all work and payment for specific completed tasks could have been offered. Some specialised tasks at national level, such as editing *Contact*, could have been paid (as they were).

All staff with paid roles, including the national advisers and the TDOs, could have been put onto short-term, probably renewable, contracts. Such steps would have been difficult. But, if equality between different roles and ways of working, the voluntary and the paid, were to be fostered, some such steps were necessary.

A complex, innovative organisational structure that did not divide people into professional and ordinary and give higher esteem to the former might not have worked. It might have been difficult to fund. But had it or something like it been tried, it could have matched PPA's implicit ideology and given the movement a chance of surviving longer than it did. It might have given PPA time to work out its ideology in practice and to make it explicit. It might have enabled PPA to get through to the outside world, clearly enough to affect the ways people and policy makers felt and thought, its essential message about the value of parents and young children to each other's growth. It might have prevented the creation in 1995 of a new identity for PPA, under the name of the Pre-school Learning Alliance.

 That new identity marked the end of PPA as such. The run-up to that date was gradual. The logo of children, parents and play leader holding hands in a circle of playfulness, equality and unity was changed in 1991 to one with a play leader with a child on each side of her: parents and other children had disappeared.

Again, in 1991, the constitution that paved the way for the abolition of PPA was ratified by an AGM and took effect in 1995. PLA termed playgroups 'pre-schools' and introduced an educational curriculum that worked 'towards approved learning outcomes', preparing children for the curriculum that they would meet when they went to school. It thus went against PPA's belief in the value of play in itself.

Some of PPA's ideas were carried over into PLA and probably more widely into nursery and primary education. PPA was both a new social movement and a new organisation; the movement survived but the organisation perished.

Reconstructing the past – PPA's ideology?
PPA never made an explicit statement of its ideology, the deeply felt beliefs that guided its members' actions. It failed to articulate them to new generations of members and to the outside world. However, looking back we can surmise what that implicit ideology was. Taking into account parents' statements about the gains to their children and to themselves, the principles that

guided PPA members in their work, the comments of sympathetic outsiders and DW Winnicott's theory of the facilitating environment, PPA's implicit ideology could have been expressed like this:

PPA promotes and supports parent-run playgroups that enable young children and their mothers (or mother substitutes) to meet their need to sustain their attachment to each other in an environment that gives each new opportunities for social, emotional and intellectual learning that can enrich their lives and, through them, their communities.

We can draw a theoretical rationale for this statement from psychoanalytic theories of human development – here DW Winnicott's. Psychoanalytic theory offers us a coherent way of understanding our intuitions and insights about human feelings that can be too deep or too frightening to be felt consciously. But as the theory deals with feelings of which we may be unconscious, we can find it hard to judge its validity. So I take examples from sources that are easier to understand. One is ethology, the study of animal behaviour. The other is Wordsworth's famous poem about the growth of his mind, *The Prelude*.

Winnicott believed that the 'good enough' mother at home intuitively creates a facilitating environment for her infant and very young child, an emotional holding that supports the child's instinctive drive for growth and for learning (Winnicott, 1965). Love between mother and child enables the child to explore and learn about the outside world. Almost two hundred years earlier, Wordsworth used everyday words to describe how his mother held him as a baby and conveyed to him her feelings about the things his eyes and arms reached out to: 'Blest the infant Babe ... Nursed in his Mother's arms ... who with his soul Drinks in the feelings of his Mother's eye!' Maternal love creates 'the filial bond of nature that connect[s] him with the world' as an 'inmate of this active universe' not as an 'outcast' (Wordsworth, 1805). This attachment between mother and child, that in humans we call love, can be seen in our fellow primates and in many other mammals. The whale calf, for example, who, unlike the human baby, can swim away from his mother, stays close to her and learns from her how to interpret the world around it, what to welcome and what to avoid.

Winnicott wrote about mothers and babies, but 'good enough' mothers remain sensitive and responsive to their older children, and try to do their best for them throughout – and beyond – the child's early years. So we can extend the idea of the facilitating environment to those early years and can look at how mothers can bring it with them into playgroups (see chapter 2):

☐ When parents' authority and responsibility and their presence in the playgroup from time to time is taken for granted, mothers can carry into the playgroup the facilitating environment that they create at home for their child. They can contribute to a collective facilitating environment for their own child and other children. Mothers' parts in managing the playgroup, choosing the play material, appointing the supervisor and so on give practical expression to this as their equivalent choices would at home. Their collective emotional holding helps create the feeling of a 'good enough' playgroup with its stimulating yet contented play (chapter 2).

☐ The 'good enough' mother is rewarded by her child's flourishing and by her child's love for her, and continues to provide, as far as she can, a facilitating environment closely adapted to the child's growth and changing needs. Mothers seem also collectively able to provide a facilitating environment for each other. Some species of whale mothers also gather in groups that protect them and their calves from disruption from outside their group (Wilson, 1975).

☐ In the playgroup's atmosphere of equality, enjoyment and empowerment, mothers can easily pick up ideas and tips from each other about how to respond to difficult behaviour, how to extend the child's experiences, how to read aloud, and so on, and use these new approaches and skills in the home.

☐ Mothers become open to new learning as their children grow: the mother's own instinctive drive for learning is intensified as she protects, guides and teaches the child. Even watching a child build a sandcastle can impart new learning to a mother and help her acquire the skill of knowing whether and how to intervene if the sandcastle crumbles. A whale mother has to continue to learn if she and her calf are to survive in changing seas. Again, for playgroup mothers, and doubtless for whale mothers, the presence of other mothers and their offspring makes learning easier.

☐ Mothers taking into the playgroup their openness to new learning can contribute to a collective readiness to learn there. Everyone should have opportunities for 'creative activity, for imaginative playing, and for constructive working' (Winnicott, 1960). In playgroups and on playgroup courses, mothers have those opportunities both to learn from others and to contribute to others' learning (chapters 3 and 5).

☐ Mothers learn from and enjoy opportunities to act with initiative, responsibility and creativity outside the home as well as in it. Young children learn best from their mothers, as Wordsworth implied and as parents believe (chapter 5). So when all goes well in a playgroup, both mothers and children are ultimately learning how to live responsibly and creatively in the world. Mothers may move on to working for the wider society (chapter 5) as their children move on to the rest of their lives.

☐ Supervisors (play leaders) can help or hinder these processes – which is why they should be appointed by the parents. In New Zealand, supervisors can stay in any one playgroup for four years only (Henderson, 1978). That lets each new generation of parents take part in appointing their playgroup's supervisor.

Winnicott was probably the foremost child psychoanalyst of his time, the time when PPA was flourishing and, like him, putting a high value on mothers. His book, *The Child, the Family and the Outside World*, published in paperback in 1964, was widely read. Nevertheless, an explicit ideology along the lines of the indented paragraph on page 136, with its rationale, would have been hard to promote. The feelings it comes from and arouses are deep. They can evoke envy and guilt in other people, even a wish to destroy something good (Winnicott, 1970). Some people might have become even more hostile to PPA than they were already. That would have had to be faced. But that might have been better than the slow attrition of the values, principles and actions that had made PPA unique.

Conclusion

These ideas are hard to put into words. However, the concepts PPA needed were around by the mid 1970s in Winnicott's published works, in comments from sympathetic outsiders and, above all, in its members' intuitions and insights. What happened to PPA shows that a social movement, especially a radical one and one that touches deep and sometimes uncomfortable human feelings, puts itself at risk of losing what it regards as precious, if it cannot or does not make its ideology explicit:

☐ A social movement, and the organisation that embodies it, must put its ideology into explicit words, as soon as it can, even if this provokes schism within the movement and opposition outside it

☐ It must provide and explain the theoretical justification for its ideology, both to its own members and to the government and other organisations

☐ In accepting money or help from anybody other than from its members, it must examine the donors' perspectives and motives with caution

☐ If it judges it necessary to introduce paid professional staff into a voluntary organisation composed of ordinary members who work for the organisation, or for the social movement which the organisation represents, it must do so with care and with imagination.

7

The impact of change

Jill Faux

The Pre-school Playgroups Association (PPA), in common with several other organisations founded in the sixties, was, in many ways, born of real social and critical personal need. Voluntary organisations had traditionally concentrated on fundraising and doing good to others. Now, with the old social order and pre-war family and work traditions evaporating, young parents, usually but not exclusively women, often with little money but relatively time rich, were trying to find solutions to their own social problems. The Housebound Wives' Register, later The National Housewives' Register, founded in 1960 following an article in *The Guardian* by Betty Jerman, The National Association for the Welfare of Children in Hospital, originally Mother Care for Children in Hospital, founded in 1961, The Autistic Children's Aid Society of North London, now The National Autistic Society, founded in 1962, were among the groups formed by parents (often professionally qualified) who had particular needs and experiences relating to their own lives or the lives of their children.

I first went to a playgroup in March 1967. I was a lonely mum in a suburban village on the outskirts of Wolverhampton. We had just moved from the north of Scotland and away from friends and family. My son was 13 months old and I felt lost and depressed and wasn't coping well. I called in at the church hall at the end of my street because I saw mothers, toddlers, prams and push-chairs there most mornings.

This was the beginning of a long involvement with the Pre-school Playgroups Association lasting over 25 years.

141

I have spent a long time thinking about why it was such an important move-ment, what it did to empower people and how it came about that the ethos and structure changed so much after those first 25 years.

To work on this has meant looking at:

☐ how society has changed
☐ the early years of PPA
☐ rethinking the structure
☐ moving towards formal accountability in the 1980s
☐ constitutional change in the 1990s.

It was then necessary to examine:

☐ how and why the organisation changed
☐ whether this had to happen
☐ whether the outcomes could have been different.

A changing society
Educational opportunities

In 1961, the year PPA was founded, only 5.9 per cent of girls went on to any form of higher education, including A levels, 75 per cent of girls left school without doing any O levels and only 7,000 women went to university com-pared with 18,000 men (P R G Layard *et al*, 1969). As a result there were hun-dreds of thousands of intelligent, under-qualified women with time on their hands, many of whom followed tradition by staying at home with their chil-dren, at least for the first few years. There were also educated professional women who were at home looking after children through lack of choice, per-sonal conviction or social and family pressure. After all, women working as teachers, doctors and civil servants were forced to give up their jobs on mar-riage until relatively recently. State-funded daycare was restricted to those on low income and in social need, minding was not concerned with the concept of early education, only the rich could afford nannies, and there was no maternity pay or leave until the 1975 Employment Protection Act introduced it at a minimal level. Many young mothers of the 60s were the children of women who had been encouraged to go out to work during the war and felt the freedoms won then were now being denied, both to them and their chil-dren, by the government's need to give the available jobs to the returning troops and by their refusal to fund further nurseries.

Controlling fertility

In 1961, the contraceptive pill became available on the National Health Service, though for married women only. This rule was later relaxed and take-up of the pill was rapid. Between 1962 and 1969, the number of users in the UK rose from approximately 50,000 to over a million. At last women had control of their own fertility and, because they were able to limit their families, were beginning to see possibilities outside the home.

Legislation, research and reports affecting playgroups

Throughout the 60s, 70s and 80s, as the playgroup movement grew along with the economy, there was an explosion of legislation and a number of government-commissioned reports intended to inform policy and to ensure that the new welfare state and organisations, both public and private, behaved responsibly and were accountable. These are outlined in the timeline beginning on page 174.

By the end of the 60s, the relatively unregulated early days of hiring a hall, fundraising for material and equipment, collecting the fees and paying the bills, often with little in the way of formal records, were over. Running a playgroup – both for the staff and for the management committee – became an immensely more complicated undertaking. I remember a playgroup leader contacting me because she had received a tax demand for several hundred pounds – much more than she had ever been paid as a leader – and her husband, who had opened her letter, was both furious and suspicious. I went with her to the tax office where we were told they were sending out demands for random amounts in order to get a reaction because they had cottoned on to the fact that people were 'working' and not submitting tax returns. This practice, I later found out, was widespread and childminders were similarly affected. We soon disabused him but the playgroup leader's relationship with her husband had been badly damaged and trust eroded.

Increasing costs

In the 70s, a time of burgeoning inflation, costs were going up, as was unemployment. At the same time the squeeze on household incomes when many women were not working meant that playgroup fees could not be raised sufficiently to meet the costs. The gap between fee income and expenditure grew each year. Fundraising became more and more important, and ultimately government grant aid at both national and local level became essential if PPA was to continue to be relevant and to work within all communities and not become a preserve of the middle class.

The need for funding

Undertaking the provision to other people of a consistent service, upon which they depend on a regular basis, requires consistent and reliable funding, something neither playgroups nor PPA could see how to achieve without grant aid – and with grant aid comes accountability to the source of funding. 'He who pays the piper calls the tune.' Other organisations, such as the Family Planning Association, found that agreeing to fill a gap in health and welfare provision led to a need to formalise, accept funding, become part of the NHS (as the FPA did in 1974) and thereby lose some of the spontaneity that characterised many of the 60s movements.

A mobile society

Partly because women could now increasingly contemplate leaving their husbands and making their own way economically, there were many more single-parent families during this period. The post-war renewal of housing stock, with new estates burgeoning in the suburbs, also led to the breakdown of the extended family and to grown-up children living away from their parents, not in the next street or next door. Grannies, sisters and aunts were no longer living near and, even if they were, they were more likely to be in full-time work than to be available as a shoulder to cry on, a source of advice or reliable childcare. Mothers in playgroups and on courses had often had little experience of children of other ages, other than their own sibling if there was one: 'My baby was the first one I ever held.' The recessions of the late 70s and the mid 80s exacerbated the situation, with many families moving to find work.

The developing meritocracy

By 1980 Margaret Thatcher was Prime Minister and her famous remark in an interview with *Woman's Own* magazine (31.10.1987) that 'there is no such thing as society' was characteristic of the times. So was Norman Tebbit's 'Get on your bike and look for work' philosophy. Mrs. Thatcher's government privatised many services previously regarded as having a social role, such as telephone and power services, and encouraged entrepreneurship and meritocracy. There was an ever-growing divide between rich and poor as competition for jobs increased. Material competition was the driver and keeping up with the Joneses could pervade neighbourly relationships.

Housing pressures

In some families, it was becoming imperative that women as well as men went out to work. This was not just because the women's movement was pushing at the barriers to employment. The country faced massive inflation, particularly house-price inflation. This was due to the combined effects of the post-war baby boomers coming into the housing market, the depletion of the housing stock during the war and the loss of social housing as a result of the sale of council houses. (The average house price in 2010 stood at roughly six to eight times the average annual income, whereas in the seventies it was about two to three times.)

By the mid to late 70s, as a result of the implementation of the Sex Discrimination Act (1975) and the work of the Equal Opportunities Commission in challenging the practice of not allowing women finance and credit in their own right (EOC, 1996:5), mortgage providers began to take women's incomes into account when calculating how much they would lend. This in turn led to a further increase in house prices.

The rush for funding

At the same time as the demand for daycare and family support grew in response to the rising birth rate – the children of the post-war baby boomers – there was a rapid expansion of the voluntary sector. As well as new organisations, such as Gingerbread and the National Childminding Association, familiar organisations expanded their remit. Barnados, the National Society for the Prevention of Cruelty to Children, Save the Children Fund and National Children's Homes, for example, started expanding their playgroup provision and developing other support groups for families identified as having problems. Churches started playgroups; schools branched out into them – both as practice for teenagers and as substitute nursery provision; clinics wanted groups on the premises in which to observe children needing extra support; hospitals and prisons wanted them to occupy the children of visitors. Groups within the voluntary sector began to start any projects for which government funding was available, even if these were different from the original *raison d'être* of their organisations, and often with little knowledge of working with groups of children and parents, or of children's developmental and educational needs. All this activity, while increasing available provision, blurred the developing PPA ethos and message and made it more difficult for playgroups to project a coherent image.

By the mid eighties:

- ☐ the complexity of running a playgroup within the law had increased enormously
- ☐ the supply of unwaged, undereducated women who started and supported playgroups and ended up running them either as voluntary or lowly paid play-leaders or as trustees was diminishing

☐ the receipt of government money directly for the delivery of a service had changed the relationship between government and PPA

☐ the growth of employment opportunities for women meant that there was more need for somewhere for the children to be looked after while parents worked

☐ the increasing pace of life for young parents meant there was less time for involvement, let alone responsible participation in management or the opportunity to become more confident and happy in their parenting role

☐ social and economic pressures left many mothers with no real choice except to work, often in low-paid jobs with long hours.

Childcare was thus becoming an essential service for some parents instead of an optional adventure that gave adults and children opportunities for fun and for learning from each other and from others. And we have to ask whether anything has replaced what has been lost.

The early years of PPA

Chapter 1 described the early years of the movement, the way in which the pioneers worked towards defining its purpose and the dilemmas around quality and standards. The proposed PPA Approved Group Scheme was discarded as it became apparent that the do it yourself model had untold benefits for individuals, and this model was extrapolated and adopted to develop a firm commitment to parental responsibility as an ideal to strive for in every group.

In 1974 the published aim of the association changed to reflect this and to state that its objectives were twofold:

☐ to help children develop

☐ to encourage parents to understand, enjoy and provide for their children.

The fulfilment of the second of the two objectives was dependent upon whole-heartedly embracing parents as partners. Just as Paulo Freire (Freire, 1972) found in his work in Brazil that it is important to situate educational activity in the lived experience of participants, the movement was, not always consciously, capitalising on the huge awakening awareness and energy for learning released by the experience of parenthood and love for children.

Crisis of management

The snowballing of activity, fuelled by the rapid rise in membership from 3,000 member playgroups in 1968 to over 9,000 in 1974 (PPA *Facts and Figures*, 1968 and 1974), with everyone learning from each other in a whirligig of enthusiasm, was producing a crisis of management at the national level. Dedicated volunteers throughout the movement were undertaking multiple roles, dealing with government at every level and trying to support and advise individual playgroups as well as helping branch and county associations establish themselves. Most of these volunteers were young mothers coping with the demands of small children, wiping bottoms with one hand while talking to Directors of Education on the phone or consoling an inexperienced tutor distressed by what she saw as her failure to communicate.

Rummaging amongst shopping lists, piles of ironing and dirty washing to find the box into which the loo roll inners, egg boxes and yoghurt pots had been gathered to take to playgroup while reassuring a caretaker that sand would not be a problem on the floor and yes, we did know the badminton group was coming that evening, was all grist to the mill. Trying to find some personal space safe from small inquisitive children for storing vital address lists and telephone numbers was a nightmare. No mobile phones then, and no storing of numbers on landlines either. I well remember laughing when letters came through my door addressed to the mailing department, the director or the publications office. In my case, the crunch came when I managed to set the upstairs kitchen on fire while answering a phone call in my 'office' – a very small table by the phone at the bottom of the stairs. My husband has insisted on a fixed phone in the kitchen ever since.

Need to rethink

Boxes under local beds were mirrored by national publications being kept in the gallery of a disused chapel in Leighton Buzzard and the lack of anything that could be called a headquarters. This was important because phenomenal things were achieved in this chaotic but creative buzz and also because anybody could do it. It was genuinely inclusive and a real foundation-stone – all you had to be was willing, and power was spread among all those beds, airing cupboards, garages and windowsills. But at national level, this would no longer do and there was a serious need to rethink the structure.

McKinsey and the development of the committee structure

In 1972, through a personal contact with a National Executive Committee (NEC) member, management consultants McKinsey offered to conduct a major review. PPA was flattered to receive this offer from such a prestigious organisation and accepted it. This review, *A New Decade for PPA: memorandum to the National Executive Committee* (Inter-Action, 1973), theoretically formalised the existing national structure into eight regionally representative national committees, regions being based on the HMI regions at the time. The national committees were: Communications and Media, Fieldwork, Finance and General Purposes, Legal and Constitution, Personnel, Research, Special Needs and Training. The NEC had been up to this time made up of talented volunteers who were sought out through recommendations from different areas of the country for their particular skills, interests and commitment. Posts such as Business Manager, Editor of *Contact*, and Branches and Area Organisers Officer were all undertaken by volunteers, as was minuting the executive meetings.

Appointment of staff

Two DES-funded national advisers (1967 and 1971) were already in post. Interestingly, just before McKinsey, Sir Keith Joseph, Secretary of State for Social Services, had announced a grant of £45,000 to appoint four development and four training officers (TDOs) and £13,250 towards headquarters and regional office costs in his 'Cycle of Deprivation' speech at a conference organised by PPA for local authorities on 29 June 1972. Logically, a review such as that conducted by McKinsey and Inter-Action could have determined the roles and job descriptions of any posts that were to be created, but the new TDOs were already in post. This process of appointment illustrates the uncertainty and lack of clarity felt by the movement at this time: I applied to be a development officer in a self-selected geographical area and was told at interview that it had been decided to combine training with development and that the area I had thought realistic (about half the size of Cumbria) would have to be expanded to cover the whole of the northern region with a colleague in Durham. When asked at the end of the interview if there was anything I wanted to ask, I threw caution to the winds and asked, 'What exactly is this job?' The answer came, 'We hope you will tell us at the end of the first year.'

Signs of stress

Within five or six years of the introduction of the McKinsey structure, signs of increasing tension between staff and volunteers became more apparent and several attempts were made to define relationships and roles both within the association and within the voluntary sector generally. The outward signs of this can be seen in the evidence we gave to The Wolfenden report, *The Future of Voluntary Organisations* (1978) and the creation of PPA's internal Staff Insight Group (SIG).

Volunteer recruitment

The quality of the senior volunteers produced by the more democratic system of being authorised by each region to serve on appropriate national committees was extremely high and many had expertise and experience directly relevant to the tasks to which they were called. However, as more and more women took advantage of employment opportunities and the maternity leave and employment protection rights now open to them, it became more difficult to secure the skilled voluntary time needed by the movement. Gaps began to appear in the committee structure and by 1981 Personnel, Finance and General Purposes, and Communications and Media committees each had three vacancies. This problem was expected to become more acute in the 1990s when it was estimated that 900,000 women would need to be drawn back into the labour market. The reservoir of potential volunteers was gradually diminishing.

Staff continuity

SIG (chaired by Maude Henderson, national adviser) led the way towards recognition that staff must play a more central role in the association but with safeguards to ensure that the value of the responsible volunteering experience was available to each successive generation. This acceptance of the need to allow more power to staff was a painful decision for the NEC but a necessary one if the moving on principle was to be maintained. This principle demanded that the role of volunteers at national level should mirror that of members at the playgroup level. Thus successive generations could take advantage of the life-affirming opportunities that involvement and responsibility could afford them, if they wished, at every level of the association. Staff were to provide the continuity the volunteers constitutionally could not, as with civil servants and transient elected MPs.

Staff role

The staff role was to empower and support the volunteers, to research, acquire and dig out information, to make contacts, establish networks, act as impartially as possible and to try to ensure every angle had been thoroughly evaluated before a decision was reached and then to ensure the decision was acted upon. I think it is true to say the volunteers sometimes envied us but I think it is also true that we, as the first tranche of nationally appointed field staff, bent over backwards never to usurp their role or authority. The NEC and its committee were always the 'government' to us and we were the 'civil servants'.

This meant that in order to be acceptable as a member of staff, you had to be wholeheartedly in agreement with the ethics and vision of the association. The covenantal relationship based on 'shared commitments to ideals, values and goals' (Peters and Austin, 1985:205) outlined in a loose job description was the basis of trust between us rather than the alternative, a contractual legalistic and formal one. This makes the first of Creech's Laws: 'Have a set of overarching principles and philosophies' of paramount importance (Peters and Austin, 1985:240). It was the moving on principle and the covenantal relationship that were about to change.

Moving towards formal accountability in the 1980s
Technological development
During the late 80s and early 90s, computers began to move firmly from the administrative departments of large businesses into the home. The old addressograph machine at Alford House, PPA's head office, finally became redundant in 1987 when the membership records were computerised. Cutting stencils and roneoing them off became a thing of the past. Although accessing the internet for information was both clunky and costly, nevertheless computers made information much easier to acquire and share.

The need to control the sudden increase in information availability led to a growth of bureaucracy, a centralisation in government and an accountability in public services in a way unforeseen. The national curriculum, testing in schools (SATs), league tables, NHS targets and a mass of legislation regulating, controlling, registering and inspecting outcomes would not have been possible without the computer. Ironically, the era of instant messaging, blogs and tweets has begun to undermine the hierarchical systems initially made possible by the technology, and the internet can now be seen as a great democratising force. Word spreads like wildfire and management can struggle to keep control. In response, 'flatarchies' are beginning to reappear.

At the same time as computerisation was taking place generally, the Association itself was growing very fast (there were 12,000 group members by 1981) and there was a need to develop more formal systems.

Betrayal of trust
In 1985 the NEC discovered that the finance officer, one of PPA's professional senior staff, had been siphoning off sums of money over a significant period

of time. This had been undetected by auditors and PPA's bank, which should have spotted inappropriate practices. Various volunteers and senior staff had had suspicions for some time, but it was the intelligent persistence of two senior volunteers with financial responsibility (the Hon Treasurer and the chair of the Finance and General Purposes Committee) who eventually uncovered hard evidence of the finance officer's long-term dishonesty. He was subsequently given a custodial sentence.

PPA was left with a hole in its finances of around £100,000 and faced a very uncertain future. Both the bank and the auditors, who had reassured the incumbent chair as far back as 1980, while suggesting that, as the association was growing so fast, it might be a good time to look at the financial picture overall, made some recompense, and the membership voted at an AGM to permit the parts of subscriptions normally redistributed to branch, county and regional level to be retained at national level for one year. In addition, a one-off bail out was forthcoming from the Department of Health and Social Security (DHSS), then the lead department for early years.

Survival at a cost

The negotiations leading to this one-off rescue grant were contingent on the Association finding part of the money required through the AGM resolution, but conditions were also set out by the civil servants that a new post should be created to head the staff of the organisation, and a system of line management established. The intention was that this would bring increased monitoring of staff activities and performance. It was argued that volunteers whose terms of office were comparatively short could not provide the continuity of professional management necessary in an organisation that had grown so large and complex, with its tiers of volunteer structure and staffing. There is perhaps a central irony here in that it was volunteers rather than bankers and auditors who raised the alarm and uncovered the dishonesty. The terms of the bail out, however, took power away from the volunteers and gave it into the hands of professionals.

The chair of the NEC indicated that in her opinion such a major change would alter the nature of PPA and its volunteering ethos forever, but the alternative was the Association's demise. The more optimistic staff and volunteers thought that the volunteering ethos could be sustained, albeit in an evolved fashion. No one wanted to see the association founder, with all that that would mean in the loss of support to playgroups.

This proposed change to strict line management ran counter to the management style that had evolved, and moved the organisation away from the community networking model where, in theory and largely in fact, the organisation was servant to the members, not the other way round.

Thus, the organisation succumbed to pressure and became the piper playing the government's tune without fully recognising the consequences or democratically resolving the questions first posed in 1978:

> Is it (PPA) now too diffuse and sophisticated, remote from the mum and her three-year-old? Should it concentrate on the single target of playgroup support on a loose federal basis? Or should it move towards a more professional conception and structure? As a further alternative, is its role that of an open, voluntary body, operating in the community and reflecting family and community aspirations for young children and parents, and 'professionalising' only to the minimum necessary for effectiveness? (Helen Smith, 1978)

Consequences of conditional funding

PPA, along with many other voluntary organisations, now became very dependent on government funding. What was not generally recognised at first – by staff members or volunteers – was that saving the association would involve losing the enabling principle. Losing this would mean the consequent loss of the self-help, bottom-up community networking approach where the trustees (the NEC) were responsible for running the organisation and managing the staff through consensus and shared decision making. Two civil servants were temporarily seconded from the DHSS to PPA's head office and a process of change, often little understood and sometimes less than sensitively implemented, took place over the next six years leaving anger, hurt and bewilderment in its wake.

PPA compromised on the title and job description of the new post – General Secretary became National Administrator – but in a fairly short time, not without dissent in the NEC and in the wider movement, the title became Chief Executive Officer and the post holder was line managing staff at national and regional level throughout the organisation.

Change in the 1990s

Two thinkers, both of them sympathetic to and concerned for PPA, had each created a vivid image of its organisational structure:

1. Maude Henderson eloquently described the way PPA had until this moment evolved a system of interlinking and interdependent 'cogs and spindles' in

her book of that name (Henderson, 1978). Maude derived the name of her book from the way her headteacher had told her as a child, 'You are only a little cog, but if you don't do your bit, you could stop the whole thing working.' And, of course, cogs are connected by spindles.

2. At the AGM and Conference in Newcastle in 1981, Vice President Lesley Webb likened PPA to a coral reef, where new bits were constantly growing, changing shape and colour, breaking off, always moving and adapting to the waters in which they found themselves yet each an integral part of the whole.

These images each paint a vivid picture of the way the organisation worked – sometimes messy but always dynamic.

Lesley Webb, while celebrating the living, growing, internally changing world of the coral reef she had described, warned against change from the outside, declaring that:

> We must be highly alert in PPA to the danger of thinking that just because we are big we must take those other big, recognised and traditional ways of running and developing an enterprise as our model. **We must not**. ...The form, patterns and command structure of a government department, industry, commerce ... are inappropriate to us; they do not fit a MOVEMENT. Any attempt to make us fit such models has to be seen as insensitive and, ultimately, destructive.

When a hierarchical line management system is imposed on such a structure, silos are created, breaking down the natural flow of information and blocking the effective but much less formal mutual mentoring relationships that enabled the movement to roll forward.

The move to hierarchy
The DHSS view was that it was an 'unfair legal responsibility' for the unpaid chair of the association to line manage the national advisers and the CEO. The CEO agreed and, almost immediately, the line of communication between the advisers and the NEC was cut and advisers no longer attended the NEC. Effectively the national adviser job description, 'to advise the NEC ...' had been radically altered. The advisers were now line managed by the CEO – although, for a while and under pressure from the NEC, a small National Advisers' Management Group did the job. Advisers were no longer free to write reports to be circulated to the NEC, or even to speak to the NEC without the CEO's knowledge and agreement. Other senior staff, such as the editor of *Contact* and the marketing manager, also found their lines of communication with other staff and voluntary members, essential to inform their work, abruptly curtailed.

PPA moved away from its original circular, freewheeling, everchanging web of communication and decision making, progressing ever outward with the playgroup at the centre. The table below (adapted from West-Burnham, 2008) shows the difference between the shared leadership ('flatarchy') structures that had been (and still was from playgroup to regional level) the way the association worked, and the new hierarchical system in which every department and section of the association was isolated and insulated from the others, and staff members were severely restricted in their ability to see the whole picture and contribute meaningfully to it.

SHARED LEADERSHIP	HIERARCHICAL LEADERSHIP
'Flatarchy'	Hierarchy
Collective	Individual
Shared authority	Delegated responsibility
Networked	Linear
Initiative based	Permission giving
Shared accountability	Answerability
Interdependence	Dependence
Initiating	Implementing
Trust	Control

New NEC members also found disorienting and difficult the contrast between their former experience of the movement and the silo existence in which they now found themselves.

The hierarchical, line-managed system imposed on PPA was not peculiar to this organisation. In fact it was becoming a fashionable way to ensure accountability in a range of organisations. Once it was in place, staff had little room for manoeuvre. Volunteers, however, in their roles as managers, policy makers and – technically, at least – employers, could not be brought into line in the same way as staff. This gave them the potential to cause considerable embarrassment to the new administration. However, their number and activities began to be curtailed until their role approached, as in so many voluntary organisations, merely that of existing at meetings in order to fulfil the constitutional imperatives of the charity.

Managing change

Organisational change is never easy to manage and to be successful requires careful planning, open communication, commitment from key players and wide consultation. The manner in which the changes were effected in PPA led to a loss of confidence by both volunteers and staff and a feeling of uncertainty about their roles. That loss of confidence undermined long-standing convictions, supported by personal experience, about the need to value and nurture aspiration and responsibility in parents. Working in what became a contractual, legalistic and formal environment rather than a co-operative one destroyed much of the goodwill and shared vision that had sustained relationships till now.

Within a very short time, staff began to feel so undermined and uncomfortable that in July 1986, field staff formally requested the NEC for a structure for consultation on their terms and conditions of employment. As a result of the consultation, two staff members were elected as union representatives and a number of field staff joined the Manufacturing, Science and Finance union (MSF). Such a step, or the need for it, would have been inconceivable a few years earlier.

External changes

This was happening at the same time as the value of play in itself was being questioned and political pressure was pushing towards greater structure and demonstrable 'learning outcomes' from pre-school activities.

It now felt as if the paid professional with a formal training and job title had more to give and was more appreciated than the volunteers the association had been so adept at cultivating over the previous twenty years. The enabling, supporting and assisting skills developed and practised by existing staff were sometimes belittled and seen as an excuse for not taking responsibility.

Ironically, at the time these changes were taking place, research was being undertaken into the way adults learn and operate together, and a variety of more flexible management styles was being developed. Within a few years, these less hierarchical systems were being adopted by major commercial companies and academic institutions. In the interests of progress, PPA was actually flying in the face of new thinking that endorsed much of what we had been doing before:

> Two towering hindrances to quality, service, responsiveness, fast innovation, and people involvement are functional barriers – vertical management – and bureaucracy. Therefore it follows logically that two of the leader's top strategic

> priorities ought to be proactively attacking bureaucracy and working at that horizontal style. (Peters, 1987:462)

Other changes in society included an increasing demand for daycare – and, in some cases, even overnight care – as more women went out to work. Many women felt economically bound to do so, though it was often a painful decision, especially if their children were very young. Parents' rights and responsibilities with regard to their young children continue to be of primary importance to most families, despite economic pressures, and studies have shown that if women had free choices, most would prefer to work part-time and to parent part-time (Gerhardt, 2004, referring to Newell, 1992).

The aftermath

By the end of 1991, TDOs were made redundant, the number of regions was reduced and regional executive officers (REOs) were appointed, line managed eventually by the CEO. By 1994, national advisers were also made redundant and invited to apply for London-based posts heading up new departments that replaced the work of the NEC's volunteer subcommittees. Newly appointed regional TDOs no longer met nationally, so the traditional mentoring role of the national field staff working with the volunteers on the NEC was lost along with their posts:

> The best way to really train people is with an experienced mentor and on the job. (Black, quoted in Peters and Austin, 1985)

How and why it changed
Review of the association

These changes happened partially as a result of a Review of the association's finance, staffing, organisation and membership services (1988-90). The Review team, initially chaired by a former NEC chair, who withdrew owing to irreconcilable differences, comprised members and staff drawn, perhaps significantly, from newcomers to the association, people unencumbered by its history and ethos, and with input – once again – from management consultants.

The results of the Review were put to the membership in 1990 at a contentious AGM in Hull. It was said that, as there were very few written and agreed policies, senior staff and volunteers found it very hard to promote the association's beliefs and aims. This was fair comment (see chapter 6) but instead of finally drafting such policies, the Review proposed instead to ensure uniformity by subsuming all local activity into one large, top-down organisation.

This desire to ensure, legally, that we all sang from the same hymn sheet was hard to argue with in theory at the time, but it indicated a lack of trust in an organisation that was built on trust, and it curtailed freedoms in a way that stifled initiative.

Amongst the controversial proposals in the Review:

☐ The proposal that the 450 separate branch and county associations should unite into one single association was passed narrowly after a recount.

☐ The proposal to have all staff line managed by staff with the exception of the Chief Executive Officer was defeated.

☐ The proposal that only constituted groups should have voting rights in the association caused uproar from those groups that saw themselves as non-profit making but without a constitution or parent committee. A compromise was reached after the NEC members were besieged by a lot of angry and upset people. The compromise was to allow constituted member groups three votes and other member groups one vote.

☐ A new playgroup constitution was proposed, by which fewer members were needed and only 60 per cent of the committee had to be parents. An additional clause allowed groups to get special permission from their branch each year to have even fewer than 60 per cent of parents in special circumstances.

☐ A proposal to downgrade the work of the regional centres was rejected.

The reconvened Special AGM in London in 1991 finally accepted changes to membership categories, constitutional changes and a business plan. This followed another bad-tempered AGM in Brighton, when attempts were made by members to open discussion on the change in the logo by putting an emergency proposal. Standing Orders Panel refused to allow the discussion on the basis that the design of the logo was the responsibility of the NEC, but Humberside still sold 500 'Save the Logo' badges to members at the Conference.

These changes made branches and counties all subcommittees of the national body – thus to a large extent, at least temporarily, disabling branch and county grant-aid bids to local authorities and curtailing their independent fundraising and publishing activities. A new body, The National Council, made up of representatives of county associations and those branches covering unitary authorities, was set up to be a consultative or advisory body with no policy-making power or responsibility. Members thus arrived on the NEC with little experience of running the organisation at a senior level and were more easily influenced by well embedded staff.

Some twenty branches and counties simply refused to be part of the new organisation. Some disaffected branches broke away to form The Playgroup Network, which aims to keep alive the ethos and structures of the original organisation.

A possible alternative

With the benefit of hindsight, there would have been a good case to be made for the national association to have asserted formally that it was a federation of local branches and county associations in which each could keep their independence, their own trustees and funding, and the ability to reflect and address local concerns. This would have fitted more closely with the ethos of an association that saw the parent as responsible and aimed at ensuring that that responsibility was echoed at every level.

Loss of independent support

Objective, independent advice giving became the prerogative of the president and vice presidents and by this time, the tradition of academic, independent-minded persons being appointed to this role had gone. Professor Jerome Bruner, Professor Neville Butler, Professor Donald Court, Willem van der Eyken, Professor A H Halsey, Elspeth Howe, Dr Mia Kellmer Pringle, Dr Penelope Leach, Dr Aidan Macfarlane, Professor Eric Midwinter, Lady Bridget Plowden and Professor W D Wall, among others, had all contributed to a long line of distinguished and valuable gurus for the organisation. For the first time, we now had a President who was an ex-civil servant, in tune with departmental thinking.

Curtailment of activity of individual members

The changes in membership categories caused great unhappiness, especially to the individual category of members. The logic was that playgroups were the members and only playgroups should be able to influence the policy of the organisation. Employees – and by now, the constitutional changes meant that anyone who was paid as a fieldworker or a tutor at any level in the association except playgroup level was an employee of the national body – were unable to vote, speak or put forward resolutions to the AGM. The logic was indisputable in theory but the effect in practice was disastrous. Staff had always accepted that voting was inappropriate and indeed unconstitutional at the level at which they were employed, so this was not an issue. But people who did the occasional paid-for hours tutoring at branch or county level now counted as national employees and were therefore barred from any participation in national decision making, their expertise and experience no longer available in debate.

Bureaucracy destroyed trust, creativity and ethos. Fear and uncertainty about how much initiative was acceptable and the consequences of putting a foot wrong were pervasive. Branch and county associations (now subcommittees) struggled with the new and time-consuming administrative task of restructuring their accounts every year into a format that allowed them to be incorporated into the national accounts, a procedure that put great strains on the voluntary structure.

Consequential changes
The National Centre was now able to claim a far greater financial base and negotiate better grants for yet more staff. Salary increases at national and regional levels were justified by the fact that incorporating county and branch associations gave the CEO line management, technically, of all the local area organisers, other local fieldworkers and any directly employed tutors.

In order to effect these constitutional changes, the national AGM had to become more managed. It became a one-day event centrally organised by staff, losing the celebratory volunteer-organised three-day conference and AGM that had always held a frisson of unpredictability and excitement as it had taken proposals from the floor and had done so much to bring on volunteers through playgroups to branch, county, regional and ultimately national committees. Motions became composites. The moving on philosophy, which had done so much for so many, was effectively abandoned. National committees were largely replaced by paid posts, and, again, pay was substantial. Where national committees still existed they became advisory to a National Centre department, and lost their power to make decisions and their responsibility for recommending policy to the NEC.

There were unsuccessful moves to dissociate the PPA house magazine, *Contact*, from membership. When this didn't work, *Contact* was 'reformed' and combined with *Under 5* to become a magazine aimed more at parents and less the eagerly awaited support for playgroup leaders, area organisers and branch committees that it had previously been. Locally produced publications were frowned upon, regional ones banned, and local sponsorship had to go through tortuous processes to be accepted.

National decision making now tended to replace local empowerment. What had been a freewheeling, spontaneous, entrepreneurial, creative and enriching movement, good and bad, warts and all, became, at national level, a bureaucratic, tightly controlled institution concentrating on standards and training. Process became subordinate to product, play became too frivolous, and in 1995 PPA became the Pre-school Learning Alliance.

Did it have to happen?

The new philosophy was that the role of the national level of the organisation was to provide services to assist the members in their task of educating and caring for children. This task had to be done by paid, well-qualified staff following a curriculum and kept on their toes through assessment. The former, unstated but crucial, aim of parental education through involvement was now very secondary if not irrelevant to the provision of high quality childcare.

Paid-for advice, often externally sourced, was now more highly valued, and more easily controlled, than the knowledge, confidence and expertise that the volunteers brought to the regionally representative national committees. One of the first committees to be disbanded was the Legal and Constitution Committee, which would certainly have blocked changes to the AGM and constitutional structure.

The association was, on the whole naïve, innocent and unsophisticated, ill-prepared for takeover having insufficient organisational forces, and indeed an insufficiently articulated ethos and purpose (see chapter 6), to oppose the move. The failure of the movement to articulate and hold true to its beliefs, coupled with the desire to influence through inclusion and encouragement rather than exclusion and directives, allowed incompatible and inappropriate management systems to become embedded and the good model principle to be eroded. The place of the volunteer as manager and policy maker at the national level virtually disappeared.

Change in other organisations

PPA wasn't the only voluntary organisation going through traumas at this time. The WEA was similarly reconstituted. In 1991:

> (WEA) districts had to discuss two models of a new WEA constitution. Either we decided to be 'Integrated' or 'Discrete'. It was decided in December, in Manchester Town Hall, where, by the narrowest of (perhaps) majorities the WEA integrated itself. (Standen, 2010)

The formal dissolution of the WEA districts was effected at the AGM in 1993 when district activists sold record numbers of a beaker at a stall marked 'Get Mugged Here'.

After much debate, Citizens' Advice Bureaux retained their federated structure of individual bureaux but introduced strict criteria and standards, which have to be upheld if a local bureau wishes to retain the brand name. This could have been a model for PPA. Shelter has moved from individual branches into a single organisation structure causing local unhappiness. Victim Support has restructured more successfully.

The National Federation of Women's Institutes is an obvious example of an organisation that has retained its bottom-up structure, where members, groups and county organisations have effectively created the Federation, which is celebrated each year with a very large annual conference – over 4,000 members in 2009. Charles Handy describes the federal organisation as:

> A reverse thrust organisation, where the initiative, the drive and the energy come mostly from the bits, with the centre an influencing force, relatively low in profile. (Handy, 1989, chapter 5)

Social and political change

PPA and many of the other organisations founded in the 60s are often broadly defined as social movements where people come together to undertake social change. The association did not regard itself as a social movement, but it did certainly effect social change.

The service levels of provision for which the pioneers of the movement fought have in some ways been realised. But this was at the cost of sacrificing some of the principles and beliefs that characterised the association. Regrettably, PPA's central philosophy was subordinated to more easily measured indicators of quality. Both children and parents have, with notable exceptions, become passive receivers of services instead of active generators of innovation.

Marjorie Dykins, as a newly elected NEC member who was later to become national adviser for Wales, was quoted in *Contact* as far back as 1974, expressing her concern that PPA:

> might lose its muscle tone, independence and freshness through working too closely with statutory authorities ... the task is to keep well-primed the pump of new, initially unacceptable ideas.

It was a warning hard to respond to at the time, but it certainly proved prescient.

Times have changed in the thirty years this book spans and changes in focus have taken place. Perhaps inevitably, some of the baby has been thrown out with the bathwater but the need for flexible and affordable care and education provision for children below school age has been recognised and funded, albeit inadequately.

We welcome all government initiatives in this field as long as they acknowledge the paramount role of parents in the intellectual and emotional development of their children. Where this overriding principle is accepted, parents and staff will share with one another the responsibility for the child's happiness, development and well being, and adults and children together will be free to grow in autonomy, understanding and the confident acceptance of responsibility.

There is a long way to go, however, before we can, as a nation, be proud of all our early years provision, and there are new challenges ahead. Acknowledgement of childhood as a distinct phase of life is under constant threat and real vigilance is needed to ensure child and human development needs are considered first and foremost in any policy decisions affecting family and work. As Barbara Castle said at the 1974 AGM:

> I see your work as seeking to universalise the child-parent relationships of the most fortunate of families, and I rejoice in it because it emphasises what I think is an increasingly important aspect of community care by which we do not so much do things for people as show them how much they can do for themselves. Above all, I admire your work because it stimulates parents to trust the contribution they can make to their own child's development. We really must not build a society in which the expert injects self-doubt into what should be good, natural and instinctive relationships.

The danger of over professionalisation is precisely that, and, although there is a lot to praise in the developments of the last 25 years, all of us must continually seek to ensure in all provision the centrality of the parent-child relationship and the active, responsible involvement of parents in their children's pre-school education.

Conclusion
Ann Henderson

Those who cannot remember the past are condemned to repeat it. (George Santayana, 1905)

The Pre-school Playgroups Association (PPA) was a notably successful organisation. As Professor Jerome Bruner commented in 1982, 'The PPA is an eye-opener. If these women had been males, they would have been running the country. No country in the world has achieved anything like it.' However, the dynamic young charity also made mistakes, and so did the government agencies aiming to support it. Mistakes are a part of human life – for individuals and for societies – but it is worrying if either an individual or a society repeatedly makes the same one.

Meeting needs
It may seem too obvious a point to mention, but the structure and conduct of facilities for young children should be built around the intellectual, social and emotional needs of children and not merely the convenience of adults or the economic imperatives of the time. The needs of children in their pre-school years do not change and are generally agreed to include:

- ☐ respect and support for their stages of dependency and for the bond with their mother or other source of security
- ☐ opportunities to engage with new experiences and to think and explore in playful ways
- ☐ secure frameworks within which they can share experiences with their mothers and other adults
- ☐ encouragement to develop their own sense of autonomy and responsibility within a stable and supportive environment
- ☐ recognition of who they are and what they have already accomplished as a basis for further development.

Many practitioners, in premises from village halls to school classrooms, are struggling to meet these needs, often in less than ideal circumstances. However, at a time when there is increasing concern about the behaviour, learning skills and attitudes of some children, focus on genuinely meeting their early needs must be a valuable investment as well as embodying a more humane and sensible approach to the children themselves.

Learning

PPA acquired and implemented valuable insights and experience about adult learning, including the learning potential among adults who have assumed – or have been taught – that they are no good at it.

The requirements for adult learners, both parents and practitioners, are not dissimilar from those for children:

- ☐ motivation arising from their own immediate experiences
- ☐ respect for their existing achievements, concerns and life experience
- ☐ regard for their own interests and for the motivation that makes them want to learn
- ☐ support and acknowledgement of the essential role of parents as the prime educators of their own young children
- ☐ open-ended learning opportunities, providing the opportunity to explore and experiment and the freedom to make mistakes in a safe environment
- ☐ basing new learning experiences on where people are now
- ☐ valuing the contributions each can make
- ☐ giving precedence to their genuine development through their learning experiences rather than to the requirements of standardised assessment criteria.

In parent-involving playgroups, the continuity, respect and support for mothers and children sharing experiences together fostered the learning of both.

Organisations understanding themselves

The points above embody the good practice that was very common in the opportunities offered in PPA to both children and adults. However, the points are created retrospectively. The insights and priorities behind them were never formalised at the time. The energetic and innovative young movement was busy doing other things, and wary of formal structures that might inhibit further creative thinking.

This is understandable, but it left the organisation very vulnerable. When pressures came, and the need to respond swiftly to totally unexpected developments, PPA found itself pushed about by circumstances. There were no defined and agreed values; no clear, shared ethos; no line drawn in the sand to indicate that beyond this point we would not go; no supporting evidence from underpinning theories. The result was a painful loss of direction and identity, and the destruction of some things that had been very precious.

Many people now feel that some of the values – and value – of PPA were eroded by the organisation not being sufficiently vigilant at all levels to prevent a growing imbalance between volunteers and paid staff. If this is so, it could have been addressed. What gave staff an increasing amount of power, whether or not they wanted it, was the fact that the constitution required volunteers to move on, while staff remained in position, becoming increasingly knowledgeable and unassailable. At playgroup level, nothing could be done about registering authorities' requirements with regard to the training and qualifications of play leaders and the resultant gap between play leaders and parents. But in countries such as New Zealand, where playgroups still thrive despite similar training requirements, play leaders also have to move on. They are on short-term contracts and playgroup parents regularly interview and select a replacement. National staff, too, could have had short-term (perhaps renewable) contracts. It is standard practice in some areas of business, and it would have been one way of retaining one of the important characteristics of the movement.

Organisations large and small have to be clear about what they most value, what they want to accomplish and how they will do so. This needs to be agreed and widely shared so that there is no ambiguity in members' minds should their ideas and ideals be put to the test.

Funding and support

Successive governments clearly admired the work of PPA and their input was at times extremely beneficial. The value for money that can result from co-operation between government and an active movement such as PPA was well demonstrated by the success of the government's Under Fives Initiative, which between 1983 and 1987 distributed £191,000 in small grants direct to groups that needed a grant. The applications were handled by volunteer panels set up by PPA, and the educationist Willem van der Eyken (1987), who monitored the scheme for the DHSS, was full of praise. The individual sums of money involved were small, but in the hands of energetic, lateral-thinking volunteers, they transformed many premises and situations.

Releasing national funding for use directly at local level like this was a generous act of trust on the part of the government of the day. They were not using volunteers to implement plans created elsewhere; they were entrusting local volunteers with some national funding, and trusting to their local know-ledge and proven commitment to spend it in ways that would most benefit their groups and their communities. Such trust always carries some risks, but it carries also the potential to unlock rich reserves of volunteer effort.

In other ways, governmental help was not always as helpful as might have been intended. Organisations, like people, need to be respected for what they are and supported accordingly. Otherwise, funding intended to be helpful can often inadvertently distort more than support. Direct funding to PPA was given by successive national governments in respect and approbation of what the new organisation had achieved, and was accepted with delight in that spirit. However, this arrangement had disadvantages:

☐ It created destabilising levels of dependency, which itself gave rise to two problems. Firstly, any organisation that becomes too dependent on outside funding from any source is very vulnerable to shifts of priority in the funding body. Money granted at one time can be withdrawn or reduced in the future for reasons completely outside the control of the organisation. Secondly, an organisation that becomes in effect an arm of its major funding body has far less freedom to go its own way. If one of its major strengths and virtues was precisely that freedom, shared throughout its membership and informing all its activity, generous grant funding can become a threat to the very characteristics that made the organisation worthy of support in the first place.

☐ Government funding tended increasingly to reward the playgroup movement for shifting away from its commitment to parent power and towards assuming a different role as a service provider. This was a pity, because independent research has shown repeatedly (eg Osborne and Milbank, 1987) that playgroups succeed in terms of children's educational attainment – and they do a lot of other things as well. It would have been better for government and for PPA if they had had the confidence to support what PPA was actually doing rather than supporting it in order to change it into something else.

The distance travelled from the starting point by both government and PPA was grimly illustrated when money was embezzled by the charity's finance officer. Professionals in finance and banking had failed to detect this, and had even offered reassurance on the subject when approached directly by the chair of the National Executive Committee (NEC). It was PPA volunteers whose intuition and sheer hard work finally exposed the fraud. Yet the government's response was to make further grant funding conditional on the movement's volunteers becoming subject to even more professionals. As a result, the key characteristic of PPA as a bottom-up, flat-managed organisation was quite quickly destroyed. The message is that the approach of supporting without undermining that playgroup staff and parents learned to employ with one another needs to be practised also by outside bodies seeking to help such organisations. The enquiry described in chapter 5 of this book would repay some follow-up, investigating as it does why and how people get involved in social movements and what is gained by it.

The facts about volunteering

A government concerned about the health of our society as well as seeking to maintain services at minimal cost will naturally look to volunteers. This makes sense. However, governments need to be aware of the facts about volunteering: what motivates volunteers, what enables them to be effective and the difference between different levels of volunteering.

Costs

Volunteers are inexpensive and can be extraordinarily good value, but they do not come free. To be fully available and effective, volunteers need to have:

☐ **Their expenses fully covered**
There is much to be gained from volunteering and it is both wasteful and unjust to exclude those who cannot afford to subsidise the activity.

☐ **Appropriate training**
If volunteers are to be genuinely effective and to have the level of skills and confidence appropriate for their voluntary task, money has to be spent on filling as necessary any gaps in their existing repertoire of skills and knowledge. Whether they are going to be chairing meetings, pruning trees or checking financial statements, the combined satisfactions of learning as they go and doing the job well are among the factors that motivate volunteers – as well as being essential for the project in hand.

☐ **Backup**
People accepting governance roles in voluntary organisations will often need administrative or other support, possibly in the form of

paid staff. The volunteers themselves, in this case, are the ones who should decide – and decide carefully, with advice as necessary – what form that support should take. There is a fine balance to be achieved between ensuring the administration works smoothly and retaining genuine power for the volunteers so that they cannot become subordinated to paid staff.

Quality

Chapters 1, 2 and 4 of this book amply demonstrate the quality of social enterprise that can be achieved by volunteers. It is essential for people interested in supporting volunteering to recognise the conditions that made those achievements possible. That level of capacity building in communities up and down the country was liberated by the absence of any top-down structure that would have obliged members to dance to somebody else's tune, however desirable that tune might have been. Members of a playgroup in the Midlands, approached many years ago by a social worker with a clipboard, looked blank when they were asked, 'Do you involve the parents?' 'We *are* the parents', they said.

What those parents were saying is important; there is a radical difference between organisations that use volunteers and organisations that are volunteers.

Either or both kinds of organisation might have merit for a defined client group, but only the responsible autonomy of genuinely volunteer groups can accomplish major growth for the members as well as the clients. And in the case of playgroups, the members are of crucial importance: they are the adults running the family situations to which the children return at the end of the day. If children are to experience real change and development, it is much easier if this does not run counter to the experiences and attitudes within their own families. In a pre-school setting in which parents have genuine power, adults and children can progress together.

Furthermore, the distinction between different kinds of volunteer groups is important because it can affect the quality of adult input – in the setting itself and also in the community outside. In PPA playgroups, and in the organisation itself, the members were on their own ground. They owned their groups; they owned their organisation. There is all the difference in the world between being at home in this way and being a guest, however welcome and kindly treated, in somebody else's home. If you are at home, you have the absolute right to be there, but by the same token you are responsible for what happens. You have a right and a duty to make it work, to make it better, to instigate changes if necessary. This combination of power and responsibility, driven by that most potent of all motives – love for children – creates the active citizens that every healthy society needs.

APPENDICES

1. The writing group

All the authors have had careers also in other fields, but this list sums up their accumulated knowledge and expertise in areas that led to the writing of this book.

Although individual members of the group wrote specific chapters, the book was conceived as a whole, all members receiving ongoing support and constructive criticism, both from one another and from our much-missed Chair, Juliet Baxter. In this way our manner of working reflected the nature and ethos of the organisation to which we once belonged.

Juliet Baxter

1970 – playgroup parent; chair of playgroup committee; branch committee; county secretary; regional secretary; member, then chair of Legal and Constitution Committee; chair of NEC; vice-president – 1989.

Mary Bruce BA, MA

1961 – responder to *Guardian* letter; playgroup co-founder; playgroup parent; area organiser; member and then chair of NEC; General Secretary – 1974.

Meg Burford BA

1969 – home playgroup; community playgroup; tutor; area organiser; county organiser; chair of Personnel Committee; regional chair; NEC regional representative; national adviser – 1984.

Jill Faux

1967 – playgroup parent; chair of committee; branch vice chair; county newsletter editor; TDO; national adviser – 1995.

Sue Griffin BA

1975 – playgroup parent; chair of committee; branch committee; team leader of opportunity group; tutor and county organiser; member, then chair of Field Services Committee; chair of NEC – 1986.

Ann Henderson BA, PGCE

1971 – playgroup parent, playgroup helper; branch secretary, branch newsletter editor; branch chair; county minutes secretary, county newsletter editor; area organiser, tutor; member and then chair of national Communications and Media committee; author of over twenty relevant features, books and publications; editor of *Contact* – 2001.

Linnet McMahon PhD, CQSW

1968 – parent co-founder and leader of a village community playgroup; founder and leader of opportunity and play therapy group; adviser to Research Committee; tutor (tutor and fieldwork, advanced playgroup, child observation courses) – 1987.

Sheila Shinman Acad Dip Ed, PhD

1959 – playgroup parent; member of Field Services Committee; co-chair Research Committee; regular contributor to *Contact*; PPA representative on OMEP (Organisation Mondiale pour l'Education Préscolaire); OU-PPA Liaison Group; European Group; adviser to Research and Information Committee – 1989.

Charlotte Williamson OBE, MA, PhD

1965 – playgroup parent; branch secretary; area organiser and tutor; founder chair of PPA/NAWCH Hospital Playroom; founder chair of PPA/Mencap playgroup; co-founder of PPA/NAWCH/Save the Children Fund national Play in Hospital Liaison Committee; chair Communications and Media Committee; member, then vice chair of NEC – 1974.

2. Moving On (Chapter 5) – how the enquiry was carried out
Juliet Baxter and Sheila Shinman

JB and SS drafted a series of questions for a pilot study to explore how those who lived through the process of moving on look back on the experience and what, if anything, it means to them now.

Constraints and limitations
These were challenging issues to pursue some fifty years on. In addition, resources were limited, and the timescale was short.

The sample
Contributions to the archive collected by Margaret Brown were an important source. Others were the *Handibooks* and earlier records that set out, from 1975, the names and addresses of all who participated in PPA committees at regional and national levels. We also used the strong personal network of friendships that had lasted over the years.

After a brief trial run, JB sent out the 'questions for consideration' to 190 people – 85 by post, and 105 by e-mail – with the option of phone contact if preferred. Five chose to talk, 73 posted returns and 56 replied by email, a total of 134 (a response rate of 70%), of which 100 arrived by the deadline for reply. These formed the basis for analysis. Subsequent examination of late arrivals reflected the patterns that had already emerged.

Analysis
SS analysed the returns, initially in terms of emerging themes and minority views, then of differences between, for example, respondents who started playgroup at different stages in the movement's development; and between initiative takers who pioneered groups and those who joined established ones. How did all these fit into the political and social background of the time? Was there evidence of anything unique about the movement?

This enquiry would not provide definitive answers, but might suggest hypotheses for upcoming researchers to pursue.

A copy of the questions used is available on email from Sheila Shinman (Sheila.Shinman@gmail.com).

3. Timeline

A fuller version of this timeline may be found at www.playgroupmovement.org.uk.

Date	Internal milestones	External factors	Research and reports	Legislation
1960				Charities Act 1960 Ministry of Education Circular 8/60 stopped nursery school development
1961	Belle Tutaev wrote letter to *Manchester Guardian*	The contraceptive pill became available on the NHS		
1962	Association of Pre-school Playgroups formed. First national conference held in London			Education Act 1962 made grants for higher education mandatory
1963	First edition of *Contact* National Conference held in Birmingham	Nuffield Foundation Grant of £750 for two years	Report of the Committee on Higher Education – the **Robbins Report** recommended the extension of HE as a universal provision for all with the necessary ability	Contract of Employment Act 1963 widely recognised as the first modern employment protection statute but did not protect anyone working for fewer than 21 hours a week
1964		LCC gave grant for ILEA playgroup adviser		Married Women's Property Act 1964 allowed women to keep half of any money they saved from the house-keeping allowance

Date	Internal milestones	External factors	Research and reports	Legislation
1965	Membership total 550	National Campaign for Nursery Education (NCNE) formed; PPA a member of its executive committee	Plowden Committee set up to make recommendations on the future of nursery education	Redundancy Payments Act 1965 DES Circular 10/65 encouraged the development of comprehensive schools
1966	First national office Membership 1500 First AGM held in Liverpool			Many more polytechnics were established in the 1960s although some are much older.
1967	First national adviser appointed PPA symbol – a circle paper of dolls – adopted IPPA, SPPA and ILPPA formed 200 members attended 2nd AGM, in Birmingham	First government grant from DES	**Plowden Report** *Children and their Primary Schools* published	Abortion Act 1967 made abortions legal up to 28 weeks of gestation Sexual Offences Act 1967 made consensual homosexual acts in private legal

Date	Internal milestones	External factors	Research and reports	Legislation
1968	PPA head office moved to Borough High Street	NCNE organised the 'Lollipop Lobby' for nursery education in the House of Commons	The **Seebohm Report** published recommending social services departments be set up	Health Services and Public Health Act 1968 set up new registration procedures
				MoH Circulars 36/68 and 37/68 encouraged co-operation between health and education
1969	First Playgroup Week	Phase II Urban Aid – £150,000 for playgroups in urban areas		Divorce Act introduces 'no fault' divorces
	Part-time General Secretary appointed	Grant from National Playing Fields Association		
	South West Region established			
1970	3rd AGM in Brighton with Northern Region established	Phase III Urban Aid	Open University took first students	Equal Pay Act 1970
	The first of 13 editions of *Playgroup News* published.		DH circular 25/70 advised LAs to actively encourage playgroups	Circular 10/70 rescinded Circular 10/65 (see above)

Date	Internal milestones	External factors	Research and reports	Legislation
1971	2nd national adviser appointed *The Playgroup Movement* by Brenda Crowe published by PPA Annual conference held at Keele. Postal strike prevented members receiving AGM papers so voting was postponed to Special AGM in June	DES doubled grant to £11,000 enabling NA appointment Additional grants received from DES, NPFA and the Joseph Rowntree Trust Overseeing of playgroups transferred to Social Services	OU and PPA collaborated on the OU course *The Pre-school Child*	Education (Handicapped Children) Act 1970 implemented Guardianship of Minors Act 1971: Women given equal rights with men as guardians of their children
1972	First training and development officers appointed First regional centres opened	Sir Keith Joseph announced DHSS Grant to appoint four Training Officers and four Development Officers and to establish three regions	**A Framework for Expansion** white paper recommended that Circular 8/60 be withdrawn to allow more nursery provision	Contract of Employment Act 1972 Local Government Act 1972 changed many local authority boundaries
1973	AGM in Edinburgh – Scottish PPA separately constituted Lady Plowden became President of PPA Membership 8,300 A new structure saw the establishment of national and regional committees	DHSS grant increased to allow more TDO appointments Consultants McKinsey were brought in to advise on PPA structure – *A New Decade for PPA*	The **Russell Report** on Adult Education validated the need for lifelong learning	Employment and Training Act established the Manpower Services Commission School leaving age raised to 16

Date	Internal milestones	External factors	Research and reports	Legislation
1974	Appointment of PPA Special Needs Adviser		The **Finer Report** into the needs of one-parent families was published and made 230 recommendations for improving single parents' lives	
	Exeter National AGM – final agreement on new aims and objectives after vigorous debate throughout the charity			
	PPA had 9,000 member groups catering for about 40,000 children			
	National Training Conference in Leicester led to establishment of Foundation Course			
1975	*Guidelines for the Foundation Course* published	Barclays Bank gave £10,000 for research into mother and toddler groups, parental involvement and patterns of support to playgroups	The **Bullock Report** on language teaching	Sex Discrimination Act 1975
	Launch of *Under Five*, aimed at parents		Equal Opportunities Commission set up	Employment Protection Act 1975 (gave limited maternity rights)
	NiPPA became independent		UN Decade for Women established	
	AGM held at Lancaster		Child benefit started	

Date	Internal milestones	External factors	Research and reports	Legislation
1976	80 volunteers serving on national committees	Petition presented to Parliament asking that playgroups should have a permanent place in the pattern of pre-school provision	The **Court Report** *Fit for the Future* published	Race Relations Act 1976
	DHSS grant to PPA £161,000 including grant to study mother and toddler groups and to appoint regional fieldworkers		First DHSS/DES joint circulars on pre-school provision	European Commission Directive 1976 on equal treatment for women and men in access to jobs and training
			Commission for Racial Equality set up to oversee Race Relations Act	Domestic Violence and Matrimonial Proceedings Act helped injunctions against violent husbands
	AGM held at Warwick			
1977	AGM held at Nottingham	DHSS grant became available for developing regions	The **Taylor Report** recommended a greater role for parents on school governing bodies	
1978	National committees regionally represented		The **Wolfenden Report** on the future of voluntary organisations	
	Regions to validate Foundation Courses			
	AGM held at Reading			
1979	Branch formed in Hong Kong National mother and toddler committee formed		The **Warnock Report** on special educational needs	
	AGM held at Sheffield			

Date	Internal milestones	External factors	Research and reports	Legislation
1980	*Playgroups in the 80s – opportunities for children* issued jointly by PPA, SPPA and NiPPA			
	AGM held at Brighton			
1981	Reports published of research funded by Barclays Bank in 1975			Education Act 1981 – The Law on Special Education
	Mönchengladbach first Armed Services Branch			
	AGM held at Newcastle			
1982	Branches in Bielefeld, Hessen and Berlin	£52,000 DES grant for 3 national advisers		1983 Equal Pay for Work of Equal Value Amendment to Equal Pay Act
	HRH Diana Princess of Wales became Patron of the charity	*Emmerdale Farm* and *The Archers* joined in Playgroup Week		
	21st birthday conference in London	Grant from DHSS was £350,000		
	450 branches and 15,000 members			

Date	Internal milestones	External factors	Research and reports	Legislation
1983	Mother and toddler conferences held in Peterborough, Bristol and Manchester	DHSS funded a consultant to consider PPA's financial situation		
	Transition from Home to School surveys and conferences held in several areas	DES funded PPA to look at the transition to schools		
	Parliamentary Links group set up	Johnson and Johnson supported three conferences on mother and toddler groups		
	AGM held in Llandudno			
	Wales PPA became independent			
1984	Under Fives Initiative started in 1983	DHSS grant for Under Fives Initiative		
	Parent Pack produced	Abbey Life funded working party on Education for Parenthood		
	Report *Learning about Parenthood – what happens in PPA groups* published			
	AGM held at Exeter			

Date	Internal milestones	External factors	Research and reports	Legislation
1985	Deficit of £80,000 declared due to dishonesty of finance officer	DHSS provided help with the deficit, contingent on changes in management	**Achievement in Primary Schools** – Education, Science and Arts Committee Report recommends LEAs support playgroups while working towards nursery provision for fours in school	Companies Act 1985
	National Administrator, later Chief Executive Officer, appointed	Article in *The Guardian* called on the playgroup movement to stir itself and work out its permanent place in society	The **Swann Report** – *Education for all* – Report of Committee of Enquiry into the Education of Children from Ethnic Minority Groups	
	Mother and toddler groups assimilated into organisation	*Four Years Old but not Yet Five* Joint PPA/BAECE statement concerning early entry into school		
	1,239 members attended AGM in Lancaster			
	National Training Conference in Birmingham			
	Statistics given at House of Commons tea party: 367,000 volunteers work 7,700,000 hours a year in groups. 11,600 support volunteers give 1,704,000 hours of work – equivalent to 1,283 full-time staff			

Date	Internal milestones	External factors	Research and reports	Legislation
1986	PPA office moved to Kings Cross Road Parliamentary Links Group started attending party conferences AGM held at Caister	Winning entries in Peaudouce-sponsored painting competition produced as Christmas cards Floral Lunch attended by the Princess of Wales Playgroup Rose developed to mark PPA Silver Jubilee		
1987	AGM held at Birmingham, where Wales PPA became independent Opps for Vol first study day National Training Conference Membership computerised	PPA/BAECE statement: *Fairer Deal for Four-Year-Olds* PPA became agent for the Opps for Volunteering Scheme *Playgroups knead more dough*: House of Commons tea party	Osborne and Milbank research confirms value of parental involvement in their children's pre-school activities	
1988	PPA Review Group set up AGM held in Nottingham Under Fives Initiative replaced by Small Grants – approx £126,000 distributed 1988-9	Avon Cosmetics sponsored grants for playgroup premises		Education Reform Act: introduces national curriculum and local management of schools

Date	Internal milestones	External factors	Research and reports	Legislation
1989	Training Conference on racial issues	Carnegie Grants for regions' schemes	*Education Provision for Under 5s*: **Parliamentary Education and Arts Select Committee Report**	The Children Act 1989 replaced the Nurseries and Childminders Act
	Chair of Review Group resigned	Operational Review Report		
	Regional reserves taken by national centre	Playgroup Aid launch at House of Commons tea party and Kia-Ora sponsors *Learn through Play* with PPA year		
	AGM at Bournemouth			
1990	25 National Centre staff were servicing 10 regions, 42 counties, 425 branches, 18,043 members, 324 overseas members and about 600,000 children	Marks and Spencer secondment to support PPA Daycare Consultancy	*Starting with Quality*: report on educational experience offered to 3- and 4-year-olds	The Inner London Education Authority (ILEA) abolished
		Kia-Ora sponsored Playweek	*Playgroups in a Changing World*: Coram Research Unit suggestions	
	Under 5 magazine put out to tender	Charity Preview of *Into the Woods* for Playgroup Aid		
	Review problems at the AGM in Hull	DoH gave PPA an additional £50,000 for small grants		
	Launch of the groundbreaking *Guidelines for Good Practice* series			

Date	Internal milestones	External factors	Research and reports	Legislation
1991	Two regional centres to close	Kia-Ora sponsored Playweek		The Children Act implemented and all groups to be re-registered
	AGM at Brighton	Playgroups and subcommittees encouraged to take up the		
	SGM agreed a single association with a new constitution	Miles of Pennies theme to raise funds		

References

Alexander, R (ed) (2009) *Children, their World, their Education: final report and recommendations of the Cambridge Primary Review*. London: Routledge

Bancroft, S, Fawcett, M and Hay, P (2008) *Researching Children Researching the World: 5x5x5= creativity*. Stoke on Trent: Trentham Books

Berman, E D (2004) It takes a lot of work to break through: being second is easy. In Curtis, H and Sanderson, M (eds) (2004) *The Unsung Sixties: memoirs of social innovation*. London: Whiting and Birch Ltd

Bernstein, B (1971) *Class, Codes and Control*. London: Routledge and Kegan Paul

Bion, W (1962) *Learning from Experience*. London: Heinemann

Black, B quoted in Peters, T and Austin, N (1985) *A Passion for Excellence*. London: Profile Books

Bowlby, J (1965) *Child Care and the Growth of Love* (2nd edition). Harmondsworth: Penguin, abridged from *Maternal Care and Mental Health* (1951) Geneva: WHO

Bowlby, J (1969 *et seq*) *Attachment and Loss* (3 volumes). London: Hogarth Press

Bray, J, Conway, J, Dykins, M, Hawkins, W, Slay, L and Webster, I (eds) (2008) *Memories of the Playgroup Movement in Wales 1961-1987*. Aberystwyth: Wales Pre-school Playgroups Association

British Broadcasting Corporation (1967) *How to start a playgroup*. TV series

Brown, J (1973-4) Survey of playgroup courses. Unpublished, Newcastle University

Bruner, J (1980) *Under Five in Britain*. London: Grant McIntyre

Bruner, J (1983) *The Functions of Play* address to the PPA Conference 1983 and reported in Contact December 1983. London: Pre-school Playgroups Association

Bruner, J (1985) Vygotsky: a historical and conceptual perspective. In Wertsch, J (ed) *Culture, Communication and Cognition: Vygotskian perspectives*. Cambridge, England: Cambridge University Press

Burgess, T (1976) *Home and School*. London: Penguin Books

Carmichael, C (1973) Where do we go from here? In *Focus on the Future of Playgroups*. London: Pre-school Playgroups Association and Glasgow: Scottish Pre-school Playgroups Association

Cass, J (1971) *The Significance of Children's Play*. London: Batsford

Cass, J (1975) Play. In Owen, R (ed) *State of Play: pre-school education now*. London: BBC

Clarke, B (1989) The Voice of The Child – Who speaks? Who cares? Who listens? Working with families facing disadvantage. Paper presented at the XIXth World Assembly and Congress of the World Organisation for Early Childhood Education. London: Pre-school Playgroups Association

Codling, M *et al* (1978) *Report on Parental Involvement in Playgroups*. London: Pre-school Playgroups Association

Coleridge, S T (1796) from a letter written to John Thelwall. In Roe, N (2007) *Coleridge and John Thelwall: the road to Nether Stowey.* Available at Humanities-Ebooks.co.uk accessed January 2011

Consortium for Longitudinal Studies (1979) *Lasting Effects after Pre-school: summary report.* US Department of Health, Education and Welfare

Crittenden, P M and Clausen, A H (eds) (2000) *The Organisation of Attachment Relationships: maturation, culture and context.* Cambridge: Cambridge University Press

Crowe, B (1969) *Playgroup Activities.* London: Pre-school Playgroups Association

Crowe, B (1971) *The Playgroup Movement: a report by the National Adviser to the Pre-school Playgroups Association.* London: Pre-school Playgroups Association; also (1973) London: Allen and Unwin

Curtis, H and Sanderson, M (eds) (2004) *The Unsung Sixties: memoirs of social innovation.* London: Whiting and Birch

Dahrendorf, R (1974) Justice Without Bondage. In Reith Lectures 1974 in *The Listener,* 28 November 1974

Drummond, M J (2005) Report on Nesta 5x5x5 Project. Available at www.5x5x5creativity.org.uk accessed June 2011

Edwards, C, Gandini, L and Forman, G (eds) (1998) *The Hundred Languages of Children: the Reggio Emilia approach – advanced reflections.* Norwood NJ: Ablex

Emery, F E and Thorsrud, E (1959) *Form and Content in Industrial Democracy.* London: Tavistock Publications

Equal Opportunities Commission (1996) *Challenging Inequalities between Men and Women – twenty years of progress 1976-1996.* London: EOC

Erikson, E (1965) *Childhood and Society.* London: Penguin Books

Etzioni, A (1961) *A Comparative Analysis of Complex Organisations.* New York: Free Press

Eyken van der, W (1987) *The DHSS Under Fives Initiative 1983-87.* London: DHSS

Ferri, E with Niblett, R (1977) *Disadvantaged Families and Playgroups.* London: National Children's Bureau/National Foundation for Educational Research

Feinstein, L and Symons, J (1997) Attainment in Secondary School. In Discussion Paper 341. London: Centre for Economic Performance

Freire, P (1972) *Pedagogy of the Oppressed.* London: Penguin Books

Gardner, D E M (1969) *Susan Isaacs.* London: Methuen

Gavron, H (1966) *The Captive Wife: conflicts of housebound mothers.* London: Routledge and Kegan Paul

Gerhardt, S (2004) *Why Love Matters: how affection shapes a baby's brain.* London: Routledge

Gilligan, C (1982) *In a Different Voice: psychological theory and women's development.* Cambridge MA: Harvard University Press

Goldschmeid, E (1987/2007) film *Treasure Baskets: infants at work.* London: National Children's Bureau

Gray, M and McMahon, L (1982) *Families in Playgroups: a study of the effect of playgroup experience on families.* Reading: Southern Region Pre-school Playgroups Association

Grubb, J (1970) Handicapped children. In Wantage PPA branch newsletter 1970, pp13-16

Handy, C (1989) *The Age of Unreason.* London: Arrow Books

Hanton, M (1977) *Playgroups: a shared adventure.* London: Inner London PPA

Heilbrun, C G (1989) *Writing a Woman's Life.* London: The Women's Press Limited

Henderson, M (1978) *Cogs and Spindles: some impressions of the playgroup movement.* London: Pre-school Playgroups Association

Hogg, C (1990) *Quality management for children: play in hospital.* London: Play in Hospital Liaison Committee

Holdsworth, R (1970) *Three Thousand Playgroups,* introduced by Lestor, J. Exeter: Devon Pre-school Playgroups Association

Holmes, A and McMahon, L (1979) *Learning from Observation.* London: Pre-school Playgroups Association

Hughes, P (1979) Opportunity playgroup. *Oxtale,* Spring issue 1979 pp15-17

Isaacs, S (1929) *The Nursery Years: the mind of the child from birth to six years.* London: Routledge and Kegan Paul

Jackson, T (2009) *Prosperity without growth?* – the transition to a sustainable economy. London: Sustainable Development Commission

Jarecki, H (1975) *Playgroups, a Practical Approach.* London: Faber and Faber

Johnson, T J (1972) *Professions and Power.* London and Basingstoke: The Macmillan Press

Jones, A (1985) Children in prison. In *Contact,* February 1985 p12

Keeley, B (1974) Playgroup phoenix. In *Contact,* April 1974 pp32-33

Layard, P R G, King, J and Moser, C A S (1969) *The Impact of Robbins.* London: Penguin

Leach, P (1977, rev. 1978, 1988, 1997, 2003, 2010) *Your Baby and Child: from birth to age five.* London: Dorling Kindersley

Lucas, J and Henderson, A (1981) *Pre-school Playgroups: a handbook.* London: Allen and Unwin

Mansbridge, J and Morris, A (2001) *Oppositional Consciousness: the subjective roots of social protest.* Chicago: Chicago University Press

Maxwell, S (1984) *Playgroups: the parent as parasite, parody or partner.* In NCB Partnership Paper 2 on Parent Involvement. London: National Children's Bureau

McKinsey and Co (1973) *A New Decade for PPA: memorandum to the National Executive Committee.* London: Inter-Action

McMahon, L and Ward, A (eds) (2001) *Helping Families in Family Centres: working at therapeutic practice.* London: Jessica Kingsley

McMillan, M (1919) *The Nursery School.* London: Dent

Midwinter, E (2004) *500 Beacons: the U3A story.* Bromley: Third Age Trust

Molony, E (ed) (1967) *How to Form a Playgroup.* London: BBC

Obholzer, A and Roberts, V (eds) (1994) *The Unconscious at Work* – individual and organisational stress in the human services. London: Routledge

Osborne, A F and Milbank, J E (1987) *The Effects of Early Education: a report from the child health and education study.* Oxford: Clarendon Press

Oswin, M (1971) *The Empty Hours: a study of the weekend life of handicapped children in institutions.* London: Allen and Lane

Overton, J (1981) *Stepping Stone Projects: the first three years, 1978-1981.* Glasgow: Scottish Pre-school Playgroups Association

Palfreeman, S and Smith, T (1982) *Pre-school Provision: voluntary initiatives and integrated services in Cheshire.* Chester: Cheshire Education Department

Palmer, R (1971) *Starting School: a study in policies.* London: University of London Press

Peters, T (1987) *Thriving on Chaos: handbook for a management revolution.* New York: Harper Perennial

Peters, T and Austin, N (1985) quoting De Pree, M in *A Passion for Excellence* – the leadership difference. London: Fontana Books

Phillips, A (2010) in *Imagine – art is child's play*. BBC1 22 June 2010

Piaget, J (1926, rev1959) *The Language and Thought of the Child*. London: Routledge and Kegan Paul

Plowden, B Lady (1967) *Children and their Primary Schools* (Report to the Secretary of State for Education). London: Stationery Office

PPA (1968, 1974 and 1980) *Facts and Figures*. London: Pre-school Playgroups Association

PPA (1975) *Guidelines for a Playgroup Foundation Course*. London: Pre-school Playgroups Association

PPA (1975) *Guidelines for Playgroups with a Handicapped Child*. London: Pre-school Playgroups Association

PPA (1978) *Report on Mother and Toddler Groups*. London: Pre-school Playgroups Association

PPA (1982) *Welcome to the Mother and Toddler Group*. London: Pre-school Playgroups Association

PPA (1983) *Welcoming Teenagers into PPA groups*. London: Pre-school Playgroups Association

PPA Southern Region (1986) *On Course Together*. Reading: Southern Region Pre-school Playgroups Association

PPA (1986) *The Handicapped Child and his Mother in the Playgroup*. London: Pre-school Playgroups Association

PPA (1987) *Notes for Opportunity Groups*. London: Pre-school Playgroups Association

PPA (1988) *Report of the Acorn Committee*. London: Pre-school Playgroups Association

PPA (1989) *PPA Involvement in the Opportunities for Volunteering Initiative – report to the Department of Health*. London: Pre-school Playgroups Association

Roberts, V (1971) *Playing, Learning and Living*. London: A and C Black

Robertson, J and J (1976) *Young Children in Brief Separation* film series London: Robertson Centre

Rogers, J (1971) *Adults Learning*. Milton Keynes: Open University Press

Rosen, M (2010) in *Imagine – art is child's play* BBC1 22 June 2010

Rowbotham, S (2004) Introduction in Curtis, H and Sanderson, M (eds) *The Unsung Sixties: memoirs of social innovation*. London: Whiting and Birch Ltd ppix-xii

Santayana, G (1905) *The Life of Reason 1* (12). Charleston: Bibliolife

Scarman, L G, Baron (1982) *The Brixton Disorders 10-12 April 1981*. London: Penguin

Scottish PPA (1974) *Organising a Playgroup Course for the First Time*. Glasgow: Scottish Pre-school Playgroups Association

Seebohm, F (1968) *Report of the Committee on Local Authority and Allied Personal Social Services*. London: Stationery Office

Shinman, S (1979) *Focus on Childminders: a profile of the first Bunbury drop-in centres*. London: Inner London PPA

Shinman, S (1986) Trends in Early Childhood Education in the United Kingdom. In Katz, L (ed) *Current Topics in Early Childhood Education*, ERIC Clearing House on Elementary and Early Childhood Education (VI) p150. Norwood NJ: Ablex

Shinman, S (2000) in Evans, M (ed) *Bunbury Childminders Project: a history of 25 years in Lewisham Borough 1975-2000*. London: Bunbury Childminders

Slade, P (1954) *Child Drama*. London: University of London Press Ltd

Slade, P (1958) *An Introduction to Child Drama*. London: University of London Press Ltd

Sofer, C (1961) *The Organization from Within*. London: Tavistock Publications

Standen, M (2010) An Uphill Drive: The Northern District 1976 to 1995. In Brown, J (ed) *The Right to Learn 1910 to 2010*. Newcastle upon Tyne: WEA North East Region

Sutherland, J D (1973) The playgroup movement, the family and the society of the future in *Focus on the Future of Playgroups*. London: Pre-school Playgroups Association and Glasgow: Scottish Pre-school Playgroups Association, pp12-23

Tizard, B and Hughes, M (1984) *Young Children Learning: talking and thinking at home and at school*. London: Fontana

Toch, H (1965) *The Social Psychology of Social Movements*. Indianapolis: The Bobbs-Merrill Company Inc

Tough, J (1974) *Focus on Meaning*. London: Allen & Unwin

Turner, D K (1982) Letter in *Contact* November 1982 p33

Vaughan, J (1981) *A Lifetime of Living and Learning*. Leeds: Yorkshire and Humberside Region of the Pre-school Playgroups Association

Waddell, M (1998, rev 2002) *Inside Lives: psychoanalysis and the growth of the personality*. London: Duckworth/Karnac

West-Burnham, J (2008) *Re-thinking Leadership: from personal status to collective capacity*. In Secondary Leadership Paper 31. London: NAHT, the Association for all School Leaders

Williamson, C (2010) *Towards the Emancipation of Patients: patients' experiences and the patient movement*. Bristol: Policy Press

Wilson, E O (1975) *Sociobiology, the New Synthesis*. Cambridge MA: Harvard University Press

Winnicott ,D W. (1957) The mother's contribution to society. In Winnicott, C, Shepherd, R and Davis, M (eds) (1986) *Home is Where We Start From*. London: Penguin, pp123-141

Winnicott, D W (1960) Aggression, guilt and reparation. In Winnicott, C, Shepherd, R and Davis, M (eds) (1986) *Home is Where We Start From*. London: Penguin, pp80-89

Winnicott D W (1964) *The Child, the Family and the Outside World*. London: Penguin Books

Winnicott, D W (1965) *The Maturational Processes and the Facilitating Environment: studies in the theory of emotional development*. London: The Hogarth Press

Winnicott, D W (1970) The place of monarchy. In Winnicott, C, Shepherd, R and Davis, M (eds) (1986) *Home is Where We Start From*. London: Penguin, pp260-268

Winnicott, D W (1971) *Playing and Reality*. London: Tavistock

Wolfenden, J Lord (1978) *The Future of Voluntary Organisations* (Report on the Committee of Enquiry established by the Joseph Rowntree Trust). London: Croom Helm

Wordsworth, W (1805) *The Prelude* or *Growth of a Poet's Mind, Book II*. Any modern edition, lines 232-281

Index